Endorsements for this edition

"This book helps promote practical work that changes the way people deliver projects in the sustainable communities sector. It is useful, user-friendly and easy to follow, full of case studies to illustrate ideas. This is the kind of work the busy practitioners of today need to support them in their work."

Professor Peter Roberts
Chairman
Academy for Sustainable Communities

"Just as planning decisions should be tailored to suit the needs of the community so too should the processes that achieve those decisions. This book advocates just that in a manner that is accessible to both community groups and planning offices. The sections on financial planning, event timescale and the final chapter, Follow Up, are particularly constructive."

Dr Katharine Martindale
Director of Cities Research Alliance

"Nick Wates is a trail blazer in communicating clear, concise and immediately useful tools and techniques that transmit energy and make you want to get stuck in. This publication is amongst a handful of documents that all urban practitioners should have to hand."

Ian Munt
International Urban Governance Consultant

"Some bo_____ _____ ____ – this one helps y__ to deliver! An invaluable tool for anyone involved in community planning."

Professor Brian Evans
Deputy Chair
Architecture+Design Scotland
and Partner, Gillespies llp

"The devil is as always in the detail, and Nick Wates' Community Planning Event Manual provides it. If you want to know the effect of having carpet in your venue, or what coloured Post-its to use, this is the book for you."

Perry Walker
Head of Democracy and Decision-making
New Economics Foundation

Endorsements for the first edition*

"An extremely useful and practical guide ... an invaluable source of very down-to-earth advice on this approach to community development."

Town Planning Review
Liverpool University
April 1997

"Compiled with great care and thoroughness. It lists the smallest details to which attention needs to be paid in order to make Community Planning Events fruitful ... The text is succinct and well-illustrated ... The handbook illustrates the excitement Community Planning events generated in the USA and UK."

Dr Meera Bapat
Open House International
No 3, 1996

"The book is marvellous. It's so good to see all those complexities so clearly sorted out and under one cover. The sequence is brilliant ... A million congrats on a job beautifully done."

David Lewis
American Institute of Architects
April 1996

"A very interesting format for getting the information across – I will be using it with my students at Manchester as part of the Architecture in the Community Unit."

John Bishop
PLACE, Manchester
11 October 1996

"A really useful 'recipe' book to help make one's own local 'menu' of a community planning 'meal' to suit one's own taste! I keep it on my desk all the time."

Hilary Reed, Planning Department
Basingstoke & Deane Borough Council
8 October 1996

"Your ideas bring fresh air in the bureaucratic world of planning monotony."

Professor Santosh Ghosh
Centre for Built Environment, Calcutta
16 September 1996

"A unique guide to the whole process of Community Planning, particularly suitable for those new to the concept and who have a desire to take action for themselves ... Clearly and attractively set out, the book is a joy to handle – the size, weight and layout all contribute to its being a truly handy reference guide which encourages you to use it. The text is simple, direct and unpretentious ... Its value has been proven in the field – most recently in Kazimierz, Krakow."

Partnership Action
11 June 1996

"Comprehensive and accessible which is crucial for communities wishing to use these tools for themselves."

Romy Shovelton
Wikima Consulting
12 January 1996

*Titled Action Planning, published in 1996 by The Prince of Wales's Institute of Architecture, London.

The Community Planning Event Manual

'Where there is no vision, the people perish.'
Proverbs 29:18

The Community Planning Event Manual

How to use Collaborative Planning and Urban Design Events to Improve your Environment

Compiled and edited by
Nick Wates

Foreword by
HRH The Prince of Wales

Introduction by
John Thompson

With the generous support of
The Academy of Urbanism
English Partnerships
John Thompson & Partners and
The Prince's Foundation

publishing for a sustainable future

London • Sterling, VA

The Community Planning Event Manual

Compiler and Editor: Nick Wates
Design and production: Jeremy Brook, Graphic Ideas, Hastings
Cover design: Susanne Harris
Printed and bound by: Gutenberg Press, Malta
Editorial Advisory Group: Joanna Allen, Harriet Baldwin, Ben Bolgar, Charles
Campion, Nicola Forde, Eléonore Hauptmann, James Hulme, Eva Nickel, Debbie
Radcliffe, Geraldine Reilly, Wendy Sarkissian, Firas Sharaf, Lucien Steil, John
Thompson, Louise Waring, Andreas von Zadow

First published by Earthscan in the UK and USA in 2008
In association with The Academy of Urbanism and The Prince's Foundation
with the generous support of English Partnerships and John Thompson & Partners

ISBN 978-1-84407-492-1

A catalogue record for this book is available from the British Library
Library of Congress Cataloging-in-Publication data has been applied for

See **www.communityplanning.net** for updates and further information

This book is a revised and updated version of **Action Planning**
Published in 1996 by The Prince of Wales's Institute of Architecture
in association with the Urban Villages Forum and with the support of
English Partnerships and Inner City Aid. Translations were published in Chinese
(1996), German (1997) and Czech (1999).
Editorial Board: Ros Tennyson, John Thompson, Nick Wates.
ISBN 978-1-898465-11-9

For a full list of Earthscan publications please contact:
Earthscan Publications Ltd
Dunstan House, 14a St Cross Street, London EC1N 8XA, UK
Tel: +44 (0) 20 7841 1930 Fax: +44 (0) 20 7242 1474
Email: earthinfo@earthscan.co.uk
web: www.earthscan.co.uk

Mixed Sources
Product group from well-managed
forests, and other controlled sources
www.fsc.org Cert no. TT-CoC-002424
© 1996 Forest Stewardship Council

*Freestanding quotations are from written statements or from interviews by the
editor unless otherwise indicated. To avoid confusion the term 'Action Planning'
has been changed to 'Community Planning Event' throughout.*

The paper used for the text pages of this book is FSC certified. FSC (the Forest
Stewardship Council) is an international network to promote responsible
management of the world's forests.

Cover photographs: *Design workshops at Community Planning Events in Woking,
UK (left) and Leverkeusen, Germany (right)*

Frontispiece: *Workshop sessions at a Community Planning Event in Pontefract,
Yorkshire, UK*

Contents

Preface

Definition
used in this book

A **Community Planning Event** is a carefully structured collaborative event at which all stakeholders, including the local community, work closely with independent specialists from all relevant disciplines to make plans for the future of that community or some aspects of it.

"Community involvement is an essential element in delivering sustainable development and creating sustainable and safe communities. In developing the vision for their areas, planning authorities should ensure that communities are able to contribute to ideas about how that vision can be achieved, have the opportunity to participate in the process of drawing up the vision, strategy and specific plan policies, and to be involved in development proposals."

Planning Policy Statement No 1: Delivering Sustainable Development, Office of the Deputy Prime Minister, UK, 2005

This book on how to organise Community Planning Events was first published in 1996. Titled 'Action Planning' it was based on a handbook on 'urban design assistance teams' produced in the United States but was adapted to include experience gained in Europe experimenting with a similar approach.

The first edition of this book boosted growing interest in collaborative urban design processes and in the development of 'community planning' – planning carried out with the *active participation* of end users.

There has been a huge growth in community planning activity internationally over the past decade. In some countries, like the UK, it has become an integral part of the planning process and new and improved approaches are continually emerging.

This revised and updated edition of the book, incorporating experience gained since the first edition – and retitled to reflect how the activity has become known – is therefore extremely timely. Combined with the website www.communityplanning.net, it will allow those organising events to benefit from up-to-date best practice and stimulate further innovation and improvement to the process.

English Partnerships, the UK's national regeneration agency, has been at the forefront in promoting innovative methods for community engagement and professional working. We are delighted to have assisted with the production of the first two editions of this important publication.

**Steve Carr
Director of Policy and Economics
English Partnerships**

End product – sustainable communities

Two award winning major new UK developments shaped by Community Planning Events.
Above: Upton, Northampton – a sustainable urban extension with 1,000 new homes masterplanned by The Prince's Foundation using an Enquiry by Design.
Below: The Village at Caterham, Surrey – a mixed use neighbourhood with 366 new homes to a plan by John Thompson & Partners arising from a community planning weekend attended by 1,000 people.
(See page **100** for project details.)

In 1996, when the original Action Planning publication was first produced by my then Institute of Architecture, community engagement still sat on the margins of statutory planning.

Twelve years later, it is heartening that public participation, once only considered relevant to the regeneration of awkward pockets of the inner-city, is now a legal requirement whenever new building schemes are proposed or spatial strategies drawn up. Local authorities must demonstrate that all has been done to engage those affected by new development in decisions about design and layout before planning permission is granted. I am proud to say that my own Foundation for the Built Environment has been a strong influence in this regard, pioneering – with English Partnerships – the Enquiry by Design process which brings together professional consultants and community representatives and which allows decisions on large developments to take place in as transparent a forum as possible. While the intensive nature of these events can be exacting, they can nevertheless secure solutions with astonishing speed, in contrast to the more usual sequential planning process. The value of early events is now demonstrated by a greater sophistication in built schemes around the United Kingdom, including Upton, on the edge of Northampton, or indeed Poundbury - which is still the largest scheme I am aware of to have benefitted from a community planning process, back in 1989. Well planned settlements command both the pride of their inhabitants and – research suggests – a market premium.

Therefore, we have much to celebrate as this Community Planning Event Manual is published. But I would urge all those who are involved in the engagement of communities to push further, taking advantage of a vastly enhanced legal position to demand higher standards of design in the built environment – the kind of design that addresses real local needs, reflects local context and enhances local economies. Reflecting local (and natural) responses in materials and building skills will prove a better bet than the standard developer product, supporting the communities in which development sits and mitigating its effect on the planet.

The breadth and variety of collaborative planning events outlined in these pages reflect the passion shared by so many where changes to our precious towns and cities are concerned. If this strength of feeling can now be channelled to provoke meaningful, long-term change in the way we plan and build, then I hope that those early steps towards consensus planning will have been richly justified. I am delighted that my Foundation is helping to publish this manual to help people grasp the immense opportunities offered by this valuable approach.

HRH The Prince of Wales taking part in a Community Planning Event at Poundbury, Dorchester, UK. Over 2,000 people attended the 5-day 'planning weekend' to explore the implications of building a new town on Duchy of Cornwall property. Over 75% of the 400 people who filled in a questionnaire thought the event worthwhile and almost 90% wanted continued involvement as the project progressed.

From pioneering to mainstream

Introduction by John Thompson

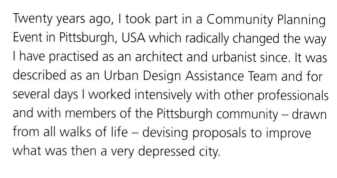

Twenty years ago, I took part in a Community Planning Event in Pittsburgh, USA which radically changed the way I have practised as an architect and urbanist since. It was described as an Urban Design Assistance Team and for several days I worked intensively with other professionals and with members of the Pittsburgh community – drawn from all walks of life – devising proposals to improve what was then a very depressed city.

Since then, our practice, John Thompson & Partners, has adopted and adapted the key team working and participatory planning techniques that I first discovered in Pittsburgh. We progressed from being community architects involving residents in designing their own homes to community planners, using similar methods at a neighbourhood, town or city scale. 'Charrettes' and 'Community Planning Events' have become central to our philosophy and we are now applying these techniques on a wide variety of place-making projects throughout Europe and in countries and cultures as diverse as Iceland, Russia and Abu Dhabi.

We believe that sustainable development is most effectively achieved if the knowledge and commitment of stakeholders is engaged at every stage of the process. A structured participatory process enables the community, the private sector and the local authority to work together in a creative way, which ultimately adds value at all levels – physical, social, economic and environmental – leading to better and more sustainable places.

Community involvement in planning
Design workshop at a Community Planning Event

"People like Marilyn came along to the Community Planning Weekend and she's still one of the great champions. Look at the amazing contribution she's made to young people's lives ... It's all about people getting involved with where they live – that is what really matters."

Bob Evans
Tandridge Borough Council

New approach to planning
Interdisciplinary, collaborative and community-based. Walkabout by architects and local residents during a Community Planning Event in Pontefract and Castleford, Yorkshire, UK. John Thompson is far left

Community Planning Events can be extremely successful both in galvanising community participation and in allowing collective decisions to be made in an efficient and effective way. An event that has been properly designed has the ability to create a unique chemistry of activity and energy, allowing all the potential players to work towards a common goal in a more effective way than by using conventional professional methods alone.

Making use of local knowledge and commitment
Plenary sessions at Community Planning Events

"After the Community Planning Weekend at Caterham Barracks we set up a series of small topic groups and through these meetings the public actually came to believe in what we were trying to do. People also came to realise that things weren't as easy as they seemed, and everything has a price as well. If you want lots of wonderful things somebody has to pay for it. For the developer to pay for it, the developer has to be making a profit. So the message got through – and that's one of the benefits of collaborative planning."

**Colm Lennon
Planning Consultant**

During the collaborative Community Planning Event process we take people up the 'ladder of participation' (see illustration opposite) to the point where they understand more about what is possible and what is not. Citizens from all walks of life learn about design and planning. Development professionals learn what citizens need in order to have a good quality of life. As a result, all those participating in the process begin to understand that the way forward is about negotiation, reconciliation and compromise. Once people share knowledge, a shared vision for the future becomes possible. One is closer to achieving consensus.

The state of the art has progressed a great deal since the first edition of this book. Twelve years ago most of our Community Planning Events were organized for public sector clients. Since then we have demonstrated that they can be very worthwhile for the private sector too.

The breakthrough was at Caterham in Surrey (see pages ix, 5 and 100) where a five-day community planning weekend about what to do with a redundant army barracks was attended by over 1,000 people. The process transformed the community's previous hostility to any new development into positive support for the creation of a mixed use scheme that increased the development value of the site by £50 million and provided £2.5 million worth of new community benefits, to be partly owned and run by a not-for-profit community development trust; that represents increased development value of £10 million and community benefits worth £0.5 million for each day of the Community Planning Event. In addition, because everyone affected was involved in developing the proposal, the scheme passed quickly through the

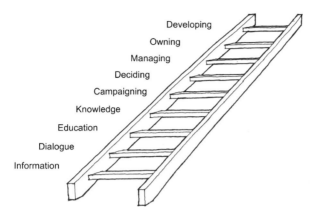

Developing
Owning
Managing
Deciding
Campaigning
Knowledge
Education
Dialogue
Information

Ladder of participation
Community planning can take communities as far up the ladder as they want to go; but beware of starting unless you are prepared to go to at least the fourth step

Engaging young stakeholders
John Thompson (right) gets young people involved in planning their future environment by facilitating an outdoor Post-it note brainstorm during a Community Planning Event

formal statutory planning process with no need for costly and time-consuming public enquiries. The development industry and government sat up and took notice.

Government commitment to community involvement in planning has increased dramatically in many countries and this is to be welcomed. But it is mostly seen as 'consultation' rather than 'participation'. The danger is that it may become merely formulaic, leading to superficial tick-box exercises carried out with little belief in the value of the outcomes.

It is crucial to recognise the difference between participation and consultation: consultation is now obligatory (in the UK and many other countries) but participation is not. Consultation without participation is simply asking people to agree with what has already been decided by others and is likely to prompt a negative reaction. Full participation, as in a properly organised Community Planning Event and ongoing process is not about getting people to agree to proposals drawn up by professionals; it is about creating better proposals and therefore better places. Improving quality of life becomes a shared goal, around which a vision for the future and specific projects can then be developed.

One of the most urgent challenges facing humankind is how to build more sustainable cities, towns and villages. Places that consume less energy, create less pollution and that are uplifting to live and work in. The quest is to identify and determine new forms of urbanism fit for the 21st century.

Shared goals
Applause during a report back from workshop groups on how to make the neighbourhood better for everyone

Community planning can play a vital role in taking this agenda forward and accelerating its delivery. The events described in this manual can produce results, and quickly. They can be used for any scale of project and the formula can be adapted in an infinite number of ways to suit different circumstances. This book will be an invaluable tool for guiding you along the way.

John Thompson
Chairman, John Thompson & Partners
Chairman, The Academy of Urbanism

Using this book

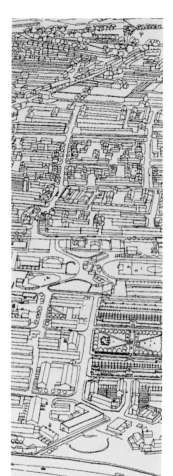

Organised well, Community Planning Events can be immensely rewarding. Organised badly, they can be a sad waste of energy. The formula is open to abuse unless good practice principles are followed.

This manual brings together experience gained to date. It is for anyone wanting to organise an event. It focusses on the classic 6-day 'community planning weekend', but the same basic principles apply to shorter or longer events.

The book has been designed to be useful before, during and after events. Double-page spreads are self-contained and include handy sample documents and checklists with space for your own additions. Pages can be blown up to create exhibition panels or reduced to form leaflets or working documents.

This edition is also integrated with the **Community Planning Website (www.communityplanning.net)** where further and constantly updated material can be found.

An important part of the process is tailoring the formula to meet your specific needs. Use the book as a guide and stimulant, not a blueprint.

Community Planning Events keep evolving. Comments from readers and feedback from events would therefore be most welcome for compiling future editions and updating the website.

Please send to:

The Editor, Community Planning Event Manual
Email: info@nickwates.co.uk
or use the feedback facilities on:
www.communityplanning.net

Modular
Copy pages as exhibition posters or leaflets (no copyright problems providing you credit the source).

| A5 | A4 | A3 | A2 |

Book Features

Checklists
Use these to plan your own events

Equipment and Supplies

Checklist for large-scale event. Adjust accordingly.

A ESSENTIAL ITEMS
for most events

☐ Aerial photographs
☐ Banners and directional signs with fixings
☐ Base maps and plans of the area at different scales (1:200 and 1:400 most

Sample timetables
Use these to understand the different event types and who needs to attend when

DAY 1 THURSDAY BRIEFING

08.00	**Setting up** Room arrangements. Delivery of equipment and supplies. Erection of banners and signs
12.00	**Team assembles**
13.00	**Buffet lunch** Welcome by hosts, sponsors etc

Explanatory images
Photos and illustrations aim to clarify the process and provide inspiration. They have been selected from a variety of events over the past two decades. Details can be found in the Photo and illustration credits on page **114**

Insights and inspiration
Quotations from a range of event participants over the years. Sources on page **116**

Sample documents
Use these to save time

Sample Briefing Pack Letter

Dear

Anytown Community Planning Event

Many thanks for agreeing to take part in this event as: [insert role, ie Team member, Advisor, Admin staff, student support].

A briefing pack is enclosed containing the following information for you to look at before you arrive:

* Mission statement
* Team list with roles and responsibilities
* Biographical notes on Team members

PRINCIPLES

* **Essential ingredients**
  Ignore at your peril

TIPS

* **Good ideas**
  Based on experience

the community planning website helping people shape their cities, towns and villages in any part of the world

"The brilliant website communityplanning.net sets out clear advice on a whole range of ways you can get people involved - using everything from models, to photos, to computer maps to show what development could look like."

Rt Hon Hazel Blears MP,
Secretary of State for Communities and Local Government
25 March 2008

Related website
Check for further information and updates
www.communityplanning.net

"I only went to be nosy. I just went to see what was going on and before I knew what had happened I was in the thick of it. I went Friday, Saturday, went back Sunday for an hour or two and then Monday night as well. I thought it was brilliant. I really enjoyed it. Very hard work but really exciting. It took me a week to sleep properly afterwards; all these ideas were springing back into my head. What made the weekend so good was having professional people there with local people as well. That was the ideal combination. Having everybody in one room together slogging it out got a lot of good ideas out."

Donna Fallows, resident, London, speaking after participating in a Community Planning Weekend (shown above with baby)

Section 1
Overview

Philosophy

Interdisciplinary, collaborative and community-based
Design workshop at a Community Planning Event

"If more towns, villages and cities held regular, cathartic events which examined what exactly was happening to their citizens' habitat and attempted to seek solutions which met with the broad approval of the public through a process which mixed professional, public and private interests we would have, I think, a much better country – one where the rejection of the architect would not be automatic and the dead hand of professional planning would be removed."

Lee Mallett
Journalist

Community Planning Events have not suddenly been invented. Rather, the technique has evolved – and is still evolving – from practical experience in many parts of the world. It can best be seen as part of an emerging technology of 'community planning' which makes it easier for people to participate in the creation and management of their built environment and enables developers and planners to use the experience and knowledge of local people to create better places.

The underlying philosophy of community planning is interdisciplinary, collaborative and community-based; enabling all those affected (known as 'stakeholders') to participate in the planning process. The premise is that better environments can be created if local communities are involved from an early stage, working closely and directly with a wide range of specialists. In arriving at the process described in this book, practitioners have drawn on experience from many disciplines including company management, human psychology and urban design.

As a clearly defined planning technique, Community Planning Events lasting 4 to 6 days (the main focus of this book) were pioneered over 40 years ago in the United States. By the mid 1990s over one-tenth of that nation's population was estimated to have benefited from over 125 events in a programme run by the American Institute of Architects alone.* Other national, state and local institutions also promoted similar activity.

From the mid 1980s, Community Planning Events surfaced in Europe. The American approach was adapted to the different cultural conditions and fused with European regeneration experience.

*R/UDAT Handbook 1992, page 84

Countless 'community planning weekends' and 'urban design action team' events lasting 4 to 6 days have now been held in the UK and mainland Europe. At the same time a variety of related initiatives have evolved, including 1-day 'stakeholder participation days', 'Enquiry by Design' events and urban design 'task forces' lasting several weeks.

The initiative for organising events has come mostly from professional institutions and practitioners keen to explore more creative methods. Developers, community organisations and local authorities have become willing supporters as they seized the opportunity to work positively with the other parties involved. Recently there has been increasing interest from national governments which have begun to see the economic and social benefits that can result. Statutory planning policy in some countries, the UK for instance, now encourages the methodology of Community Planning Events but does not yet specify when or how they should be organised.

In the meantime, events continue to be organised on an ad-hoc basis and the number of enthusiasts grows. An extraordinary feature of the Community Planning Event phenomenon is the way that people who have experienced one become convinced of their value.

There is still much systematic evaluation and refinement needed. But those involved in the development of this relatively new activity are confident it will come to play a major role in the future planning and management of human settlements worldwide.

Uses for Community Planning Events

- **City futures**
  Devising new visions for the future of a city or region

- **Regeneration strategies**
  For declining industrial or inner city areas

- **Sustainable development strategies**
  Developing strategies for sustainable development in the light of global warming

- **Traffic solutions**
  Resolving congestion in historic town centres or exploring new transport options

- **Site proposals**
  Devising and testing development proposals for sites or buildings

- **Building design**
  Exploring design options for historic or new buildings

- **New towns**
  Exploring the best way of building major new settlements or integrating new development with old

- **Development plans**
  Involving the public in the early stages of preparing statutory development plans

You are invited to a

COMMUNITY PLANNING WEEKEND

Enquiry by Design

REINVIGORATE

Stakeholder Participation Day

COLLABORATIVE DESIGN WORKSHOP

"I cannot think of another opportunity where such lengthy meetings can take place amongst experts in their own fields discussing issues to their bitter conclusion. This is incredibly stimulating since thought processes build on themselves exponentially and realistic solutions to seemingly impossible problems become apparent."

Michael Baynes
Development Surveyor

Key features of Community Planning Events

There are several common types of Community Planning Event and a variety of labels have been used to describe them. Common features are:

- **Thorough preparation**
  Careful planning and organisation involving all key stakeholders.

- **Intensive work**
  A fast-paced, intensive programme of work sessions – lasting for one or several days and sometimes spanning a weekend.

- **Community participation (not just consultation)**
  Everyone affected is encouraged to be involved in developing and exploring ideas and options.

- **Broad mission**
  All the problems and opportunities of a particular site, neighbourhood, city or region are examined in a holistic manner with minimum preconceptions.

- **Multidisciplinary teamwork**
  People from all relevant disciplines and trades work closely together in a hands-on, non-hierarchical way.

- **Expert facilitation**
  Events are mostly run by experienced, usually independent, facilitators. This helps provide a neutral forum for debate and confidence in the outcome.

- **High-profile communication**
  Events are highly publicised to ensure that everyone has the opportunity to get involved and that results are widely disseminated. They normally end with a public presentation and written report.

- **Rapid and ongoing feedback**
  Results are fed back to those participating and the wider public as quickly as possible and an ongoing relationship is established.

- **Flexibility**
  The process can easily be adjusted to suit the needs of each particular community both during preparation and during the event.

Holistic vision
Illustrative masterplan for a new development to regenerate Caterham Barracks, Surrey, conceived and drawn up by John Thompson & Partners during a Community Planning Event and ongoing public participation.
Top: site as then existing

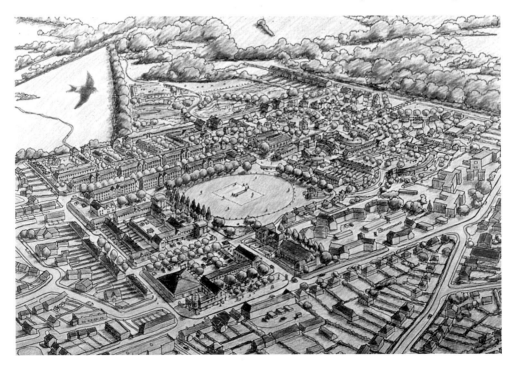

Benefits of Community Planning Events

Heightened public awareness
Walkabout during a Community Planning Event

"The process can make a significant contribution to the designing of a new development, delivering a much higher environmental, social and economic performance than has been the case of development over the past 60 years or so. Typically the process can achieve in one week a design vision that would normally have taken two years to achieve in the conventional planning system. This is due to the process being simultaneously interactive rather than the sequentially reactive process of the current system."

The Prince's Foundation

Community Planning Events can achieve objectives which are hard to achieve in any other way. These include:

- **Creation of shared visions** for a community's future and identification of long- and short-term strategies for implementing them.

- **Catalyst for action** of all kinds by releasing blockages in the development process.

- **Resolution of complex problems** or at least a clearer identification of issues and goals.

- **Revitalisation of local networks** for community development.

- **Fostering of consensus building** among different interest groups leading to better integration and long-term partnerships.

- **Promotion of urban design capability** of local agencies and improvement of environmental standards.

- **Heightened public awareness** of development issues resulting from the provision of an open forum for debate.

- **Morale boost** for all those involved as a result of experiencing team working.

Typical Outcomes

- Identification of issues and opportunities
- Agreed objectives and achievable targets
- Visions for an area's future
- Agendas for action and action plans
- Proposals for a particular site or programme
- Suggestions for organisational changes
- Local coalitions and leadership

Typical Products

Immediate
Proposals for action set out in:
- Broadsheet and press release
- Illustrated report
- Exhibition
- Presentation (generally Powerpoint)
- Project website

Short term
- Local steering committees to follow up
- Periodic progress reports
- Draft development brief and/or draft tender
- Ongoing community forums to develop further ideas

Long term
- Ongoing programme of implementation
- Evaluation of the impact of the event

Community Planning Events are NOT:

- A substitute for a statutory planning framework.
- A substitute for long-term participatory programmes.
- A technique for consultation only; it is a participatory process.
- A way of replacing services of local professionals and officials.
- A way of imposing ideas on a community from outside.

Why Community Planning Events work

Community Planning Events 'work' because the process combines a unique mix of ingredients which respond to the complexity of today's development issues:

- **Open community involvement**
  There is scope for all members of the community, including minorities, to participate in a wide variety of ways. This can lead to a new sense of cohesion and consensus on goals, the formation of new partnerships and the development of a sense of equity and trust.

- **Creative working methods**
  Professionals of all disciplines work in a hands-on manner with each other and with non-professionals in a neutral environment. This breaks down conventional professional boundaries and fosters understanding between people which can be magnetic; releasing spirit, humour, imagination, positive thinking and collective creativity.

- **Dynamism**
  The carefully structured timetable creates a focus of public attention and provides deadlines for results. A critical mass of activity is generated creating momentum for change.

Sense of equity and trust
Post-it board at a Community Planning Event

"I know from my own experience that Community Planning Events can create a shared vision for regeneration and bring innovative solutions from the people who have to live with the effects. They instill a sense of ownership ensuring that the outcomes are more sustainable."

David Taylor
First Chief Executive
English Partnerships

- **Local expertise**
  Participation by local residents, businesses and professionals ensures that the whole process is embedded in the local context and runs smoothly. Inside knowledge of the urban or rural context is essential for a successful planning process.

- **Fresh thinking**
  The intensive and collaborative process provides an opportunity for new ideas and new ways of working which can overcome past divisions and indecision. So previously unimagined proposals can emerge.

- **Visual approach**
  The use of urban design techniques of drawing and model-making provides an easily accessible way for people to think about, and communicate, visions for their community's future.

- **Realism**
  The process addresses the physical, natural, social and economic environments as they are – rather than as abstract concepts – and ensures that the community's real concerns are placed on the agenda.

Unique chemistry
Professionals, local residents, politicians and developers take time off for group photographs

Community Planning Event

What the four main parties involved do during the four phases

"It's a fantastic way of putting a major scheme together and could revolutionise the way we do commercial development."

**Barry Wick
developer**

PARTIES

		Getting Started ▶ 1–2 months*
Local Interests Individuals and organisations		• Stimulate action • Establish Steering Group and Host (see below)
Steering Group/ Host/Organiser Main enthusiasts and technical advisors		• Formation/appointment • Explore options for action • Prepare proposal • Stimulate action • Secure commitment from all affected parties • Raise funds • Commitment to proceed
Facilitators and Event Team Specialists from complementary disciplines		• Provide advice
Support Bodies International, national and regional organisations		• Supply general information and advice • Evaluation visit if requested

*Timescales
Community Planning Events can be of varying lengths but the process remains more or less the same. The length of the event and the lead times will be determined by the nature of the issues faced and the extent and capacity of existing local networks. Timescales

process
of any event

PHASES

Preparation ▶	The Event ▶	Follow-up ▶
2–4 months*	several days*	ongoing*
• Build momentum, enthusiasm and expectation through discussion and by focussing attention on the main issues	• Participate in public sessions	• Analyse proposals • Develop support for strategies and projects • Apply pressure for implementation • Ongoing participation
• Select Team Chairperson, Team members, Advisors and consultants • Establish administration • Identify key stakeholders • Prepare publicity strategy • Prepare venues • Publicise	• Event management and administration	• Assess proposals and prioritise • Agree plan of action • Publicity • Spearhead and coordinate implementation • Maintain momentum
• Homework on the locality and the Community Planning process • Reconnaissance visit (by Chairperson at least) • Warm up events in local communities and with special groups	• Arrive • Reconnaissance • Briefings • Topic workshops or plenary • Design workshops • Brainstorm • Prepare proposals • Presentation • Leave	• Revisit and assist as requested
• Supply detailed information and contacts	• Observe • Participate • Assist if asked	• Monitor and evaluate • Assist if asked

shown above have been found to be the most effective for major urban design issues of, say, a neighbourhood or city. Compressed timescales work well for simpler issues such as making proposals for a single site. Shorter lead times are possible where local networks are well developed. Longer lead times can be useful for building community capacity. (See also *Flowchart perspectives* on page **104**.)

Organising
Steering Group meeting for key stakeholders to prepare for a
Community Planning Event (top); organiser's team meeting (bottom)

Section 2
Getting started

Taking the plunge

Mission
Post-it board at a Community Planning Event. Citizens express what their neighbourhood needs

"The huge amount of effort invested in this weekend has paid dividends. The event has not only resulted in a coherent vision for Hulme 5 (housing estate), but has also shifted entrenched attitudes and ploughed through prejudice. Hulme will never be the same again – and neither will those who attended."

Lesley Whitehouse regeneration company Chief Executive

Here are 8 things to do before deciding to hold a Community Planning Event:

☐ **1** Read right through this manual to understand what will be involved. Check other sources (see *Publications and sources,* page **92**, and the *Publications & Films A–Z* on **www.communityplanning.net**).

☐ **2** Discuss it with people who have done it before and organisations that might provide support (see *Contacts,* page **94** and the *Contacts A–Z* and *Case Studies* on **www.communityplanning.net**).

☐ **3** Form a Steering Group to oversee the event. This should reflect the community's diversity and include all main enthusiasts and key players.

☐ **4** Think through what kind of event is likely to be most suitable for the issues you face. Use the Community Planning Event planner on page **108**. Consider holding a Process Planning session with key stakeholders (see *Methods A–Z* on **www.communityplanning.net**). Consider appointing an experienced consultant to assist you with this.

☐ **5** Prepare budget estimates and a funding strategy (see *Funding* page **20**).

☐ **6** Write a 'mission statement' setting out the objectives and how and by whom they are going to be achieved (see samples on next page).

☐ **7** Decide whether to hold an event under the umbrella of a regional, national or even international organisation (see *Support bodies* page **18**).

☐ **8** Check whether you have, or can you be sure of getting:

    ☐ keen Steering Group, Host and organiser?
    ☐ enough funding or support in kind?
    ☐ experienced facilitators and technical experts?
    ☐ clear and achievable mission statement?
    ☐ capability to follow up afterwards?

If the answer is yes, **go for it**. If not think again.

Sample Mission Statements

New Visions for Anytown

Anytown is suffering from a number of difficulties caused by the decline of traditional industries and lack of investment for housing maintenance. There is high unemployment, homelessness, a number of derelict sites in the town centre and a general sense of uncertainty and despondence. Several solutions have been put forward over recent years but little action has taken place because of lack of agreement on priorities and lack of funds.

It is proposed to organise a Community Planning Event next spring. The objective is to create a new vision for the town by inviting all members of the community to explore possible options with a team of specialists from elsewhere. A programme of long- and short-term action will be drawn up. A 4-day event is proposed spanning the weekend before Easter. This fits in well with the town council's deadline for a response to developers' proposals for some of the town centre derelict sites and a conference a month later on new initiatives for sustainability in the town.

The event is being organised by the Anytown Environment Network in association with the National Urban Trust. It is supported by Anytown Council and the Anytown Chamber of Commerce. Sponsors include Shell and Greenpeace. Architects Company, which has considerable experience of Community Planning, will be engaged to provide the administration and a technical support team will be provided by Anytown College Urban Design Department. The National Urban Trust will assist with assembling the Team of specialists and will monitor progress after the event has taken place.

Anyvillage Traffic Management

Increased traffic in Anyvillage is causing problems for residents and traders alike. Parking is hard to find and there have been several unpleasant incidents involving abuse and even violence on one occasion. Proposals by the local planning department for new car parks have been widely opposed.

Anyvillage parish council proposes to hold a 1-day Community Planning Event to explore some options. The event will take place during the day and evening to ensure that everyone who wants to has an opportunity to take part. A Team of transport and urban design specialists will facilitate the event and make recommendations. In preparing for the event, the parish council is being assisted by the village school, which is making a model, and officers from the county council planning department. Support and advice is also being provided by the national Civic Trust.

Organisation

Community Planning Events may be initiated by any individual or organisation. Once the idea has taken root there are various organisational models but most fit within a standard structure (shown on facing page).

Building partnerships
Producing a sheet of notepaper is a good way to think through how to position the event

"A proper charrette brings into being a collective intelligence … And it does this with stunning efficiency. No one should waste their time. No one should feel stymied. The negotiations should take place – not during the adversarial circumstances of the municipal hearing when the plan is already fixed – but during the ongoing creation of the plan, when most plan components are at the maximum pitch of flexibility."

Andrès Duany, Foreword,
The Charrette Handbook

PRINCIPLES

- Existing participation mechanisms should be built on but a new single-minded organisational mechanism should be created for the event.

- Ultimate responsibility for hosting the event should be taken by a single organisation but this will often be on behalf of a partnership of relevant interests, usually formalised as a Steering Group. The Host may appoint an experienced Organiser.

- A Team of independent specialists should be appointed to take responsibility for facilitating the event and making recommendations afterwards. Team members may be from a regular consultancy or be individually handpicked. They may be paid or be volunteers.*

- The Team Chairperson should be carefully selected. He or she may wish to work with a core group with previous experience of working together. During the event, the Team Chairperson should be in sole charge.

TIPS

- Invite non-independent specialists (eg local planners and community leaders) to participate as Advisors rather than Team members. Otherwise the validity of the recommendations may be jeopardised.

* It used to be common practice, particularly in America, for Team members to receive expenses only and to agree not to accept commissions arising from their recommendations. But the process is increasingly becoming part of standard professional work practice with Team members being paid fees accordingly. Both approaches have their strengths. The important thing is to have clear and open policies.

Organisation framework

Working arrangements for
a Community Planning Event

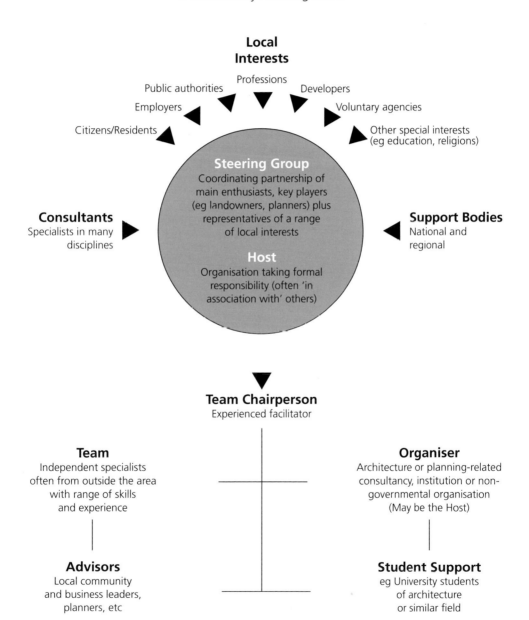

Local Interests

Professions

Public authorities   Developers

Employers   Voluntary agencies

Citizens/Residents   Other special interests
(eg education, religions)

Steering Group
Coordinating partnership of
main enthusiasts, key players
(eg landowners, planners) plus
representatives of a range
of local interests

Consultants
Specialists in many
disciplines

Support Bodies
National and
regional

Host
Organisation taking formal
responsibility (often 'in
association with' others)

Team Chairperson
Experienced facilitator

Team
Independent specialists
often from outside the area
with range of skills
and experience

Organiser
Architecture or planning-related
consultancy, institution or non-
governmental organisation
(May be the Host)

Advisors
Local community
and business leaders,
planners, etc

Student Support
eg University students
of architecture
or similar field

Support bodies

National facilitator
Charles Zucker, employed for many years by the American Institute of Architects to help communities organise Community Planning Events

"In many ways, the process has transformed the way that Americans shape community development policies and take those actions that most directly affect their community's growth or change."

American Institute of Architects

Community Planning Events often benefit from being supported by a national or regional organisation. Some organisations, particularly in the United States, have institutionalised their support into recognisable programmes.

Support bodies can provide:

PRINCIPLES

- **Advice** on the most suitable type of event based on experience.

- **Stimulation** of interest by provision of briefing material and speakers.

- **Validation** of the event which can be invaluable in overcoming scepticism at local level.

- **Assistance** with practicalities such as Team selection (by maintaining databases of talent) or Team briefing.

- **Organisation** of anything from an initial meeting to an entire event.

- **Momentum** ensuring that follow-up takes place.

TIPS

- Support bodies are in a good position to promote good practice by negotiating certain standards as the price of their involvement. The standards will vary from one organisation to another.

- Support bodies can play a vital role in developing new approaches by proactively encouraging and even organising pilot events and pilot programmes. But make sure there are resources to document and disseminate the results or it will be a wasted effort

See page **94** for details of some support bodies.

Types of Support Body

- **Professional groups**
  Institutes of architecture, planning or urban design for instance. Some have a special unit for Community Planning Events with a coordinator and committee (called 'Oversight Committee' in the USA)

- **Universities and colleges**
  Some have a special unit. More likely to be a sporadic activity of a Department such as Architecture or Planning

- **Local government**
  Can be part of the work of a planning or other department

- **Regeneration agencies**
  As part of the work of a development trust or other special agency

- **Consultancies**
  Support may be provided by private consultants who have developed the expertise in house

- **Partnerships of agencies**
  A special unit may be established by a group of organisations, particularly at regional level

Requirements

Before getting involved in a local event, most support agencies will want the following information from the event's proposers:

- ☐ Nature of the proposers
- ☐ Brief description of community
- ☐ Statement of current problems and background
- ☐ Objectives of proposed event
- ☐ Budget estimates
- ☐ Statement of commitment from local sponsors
- ☐ Letters of support for the concept from various sections of the community
- ☐ Statement of commitment from the promoters to follow up the event
- ☐ Any helpful photos or other illustrative material
- ☐ ....
- ☐ ....
- ☐ ....

Funding

Community Planning Events can be designed for a range of budgets. But insufficient funds for the type of event you decide on can lead to a failure to generate the critical mass of energy necessary for success. Establishing realistic budgets and securing enough money – or support in kind – is therefore very important.

Value for money
Tower block demolition. Community Planning Events may appear expensive at first sight, but the cost of getting the planning process wrong can be astronomical

"The process demonstrated that urban planning and design issues can be clarified and defined in a very short period of time and involve extensive and direct community participation. With continuing fine-tuning and staff resource support, it is possible to move this programme from its pilot status and incorporate it formally into the City's planning processes."

Kenneth Topping
Director of Planning
Los Angeles

PRINCIPLES

- Funding should come from as many sources as possible. This encourages commitment to a partnership approach from the start and avoids charges of vested interest. If single source funding is inevitable, the need for a validating body will be greater.

- There are many opportunities for securing financial sponsorship and support in kind, particularly if the event is high-profile and enthusiastically supported by the community.

TIPS

- Think twice before doing an event 'on the cheap'. It is most likely to lead to bitterness and recrimination. It is better to have a shorter, well-funded event than a longer, badly funded one. Always allocate funding for follow-up.

- If you find it hard to get enough funding and support, try holding a 1-day event first with a view to generating interest in a longer one later.

- To avoid resentment and/or manipulation, be clear and honest about what is being paid for and what is not.

Event Costs

Checklist for preparing rough budget estimates

Budget heading	Assumptions	£/$
☐ Evaluation visit (travel, expenses)	....	....
☐ Reconnaissance by Chairperson (travel, expenses)	....	....
☐ Transport (Team members)	....	....
☐ Accommodation (Team members and organisers)	....	....
☐ Venues (rent and insurance)	....	....
☐ Organisers/administration	....	....
☐ Facilitators' fees	....	....
☐ Team members' fees	....	....
☐ Equipment hire and technical support	....	....
☐ Publicity, advertising, stationery	....	....
☐ Catering (Team meals plus snacks for all)	....	....
☐ Car/van/bus rental	....	....
☐ Secretarial (word processing)	....	....
☐ Report printing	....	....
☐ Follow-up (team revisit, publicity)	....	....
☐ Sundries (supplies, telephone) and contingency	....	....
....	....	....
....	....	....
....	....	....
Totals		....

Funding Sources

☐ Local and central government
☐ Local and national businesses
☐ Local and national charities and NGOs
☐ Developers and landowners
☐ Development agencies
☐ Community groups
☐ Arts funding bodies
☐ Professional institutes
☐ ....
☐ ....

Support-in-kind Ideas

☐ Hoteliers   Rooms
☐ Printers   Printing
☐ Consultants   Admin
☐ Property owners   Premises
☐ Colleges   Students
☐ Businesses   Meals
☐ Bus companies   Transport
☐ Local press   Advertising
☐ Residents   Lodgings
☐ ....

Setting the stage
Banners help people to orientate themselves and provide a useful backdrop for photographs

Section 3

Preparation

Managing

Good management is essential. Events must run like clockwork or energy will be dissipated and the results will be poor. Whether an event is organised by paid staff or by volunteers the principles are the same.

Fusing agendas
Cartoonist's perspective on an event in Germany

"The impact of the R/UDAT (Community Planning) programme on the (American) nation's cities is unequalled by any other design activity over the past decade. No consultant organisation has worked so closely with so many communities. No government agency has dealt with such a rich variety of issues. The breadth, quantity and quality of experienced talent in the R/UDAT process exists in no institution or in any consultant organisation."

Peter Batchelor
David Lewis
authors

PRINCIPLES

- Once a decision has been made to proceed, responsibility for all preparation tasks should be determined (see checklist opposite).

- Clear guidelines about the nature of the event should be produced so that everyone knows where they stand.

TIPS

- Don't set a date until you are sure you can meet it but announce the date and venue as early as you can so that it gets logged in people's diaries.

- Fast-track events are possible but having a comfortable lead time is useful to allow people to prepare properly. Avoid holiday periods and major local attractions. Best to be 'the main show in town'.

- Be clear about the extent of participation and who can be involved when. Don't pretend there is an open agenda if in fact decisions have already been made.

- Avoid being unduly influenced! You may be lobbied from all sides by people promoting their own interests. Make it clear that the event is open to all and that the process is neutral, not 'fixable'. Suggest people make their case at the event.

Typical Tasks

4–6 months before

- [ ] Establish Steering Group and Host
- [ ] Decide nature of event
- [ ] Approach support body and organiser
- [ ] Secure funding
- [ ] Secure support in principle locally
- [ ] Decision to go ahead
- [ ] Establish administration
- [ ] Inform local grapevines
- [ ] Establish project website
- [ ] ....

2–3 months before

- [ ] Select Team Chairperson
- [ ] Start information gathering
- [ ] Secure venue
- [ ] Fix dates of event
- [ ] Prepare timetable
- [ ] Invite Team members (letter)
- [ ] Contact speakers (letter)
- [ ] Book accommodation
- [ ] ....

1 month before

- [ ] Make reconnaissance visit
- [ ] Start publicity
- [ ] Send out invitations
- [ ] Make staff arrangements
- [ ] Hire and assemble equipment
- [ ] Organise crèche
- [ ] Arrange refreshments
- [ ] ....

2 weeks before

- [ ] Place advertisements in press
- [ ] Assemble stationery & equipment
- [ ] Make banners
- [ ] Check insurance
- [ ] Check transport arrangements
- [ ] Send out briefing packs
- [ ] ....

Team Chairperson Qualities

- [ ] Experience of previous Community Planning Events, preferably as Team member
- [ ] Leadership qualities
- [ ] Sensitivity and ability to draw people out
- [ ] Understanding of urban design processes
- [ ] Ability to orchestrate action
- [ ] Toughness (may have to ask someone to leave the Team or deal with troublemakers)
- [ ] ....
- [ ] ....
- [ ] ....

Reconnaissance Visit

One month before the event, the Chairperson should check the following:

- [ ] Budget
- [ ] Venues
- [ ] Publicity
- [ ] Printing schedules
- [ ] Computer and photo arrangements
- [ ] Information gathering progress
- [ ] Briefing pack
- [ ] Report format
- [ ] Equipment
- [ ] ....
- [ ] ....
- [ ] ....

Motivating people

Community Planning Events are likely to be most successful if there is widespread support and involvement from the outset. Often this will require imaginative promotion because it is still an unusual approach which people may not be used to.

Streetlamp banner
Something interesting is happening ....

"This process allows the members of the community to take a proactive role in the development of their community instead of the reactionary role usually associated with public hearings and the like. Events like this are our chance to bring the community, the developers and the city, county and the state agencies also the elected officials together to formulate a shared vision for an area."

Tom Bradley
Mayor of Los Angeles

PRINCIPLES

- All sections of the community should be involved, particularly the key decision-makers (eg councillors, council officers, developers).

- Local groups should be encouraged to get their own members involved but should not be relied on to do so. The organisers must ensure that everyone – including the 'hard to reach' – has the opportunity to be involved.

- The event should be promoted as an exciting and enjoyable opportunity, not a duty. People should take part because they want to not because they feel they ought.

TIPS

- Be prepared for some hostility from people who resent you treading on what they see as their patch. Overcome it by using past examples, talking through the process and being open to their involvement; these people can often become your main supporters.

- Get out in the community. Meetings or workshops at an early stage with specific groups can be useful for informing people about the process and identifying issues. Keep them as informal and open-ended as possible. Consider also a newsletter, website, site office, advertising hoarding and any special communication methods appropriate to the specific community.

- Invite key interest groups and individuals by letter. Also make as much personal contact as possible.

- An up-to-date database of contacts is essential.

- Style is important. Develop a lively, straightforward, friendly design style and encourage a casual yet professional approach from the outset.

- Don't be afraid to state clearly that the most effective motivation for involvement is enlightened self-interest.

- See also *Publicity*, page **34**.

Groups to Involve

- [ ] Chambers of commerce
- [ ] Churches
- [ ] Community and voluntary organisations
- [ ] Developers and real-estate professionals
- [ ] Environmental and civic groups and societies
- [ ] Ethnic and cultural groups
- [ ] Friends and neighbours
- [ ] Investors
- [ ] Landowners
- [ ] Local business people
- [ ] Local councils, politicians and administrators
- [ ] Local disability organisations
- [ ] Media (local and regional)
- [ ] Planners and planning committees
- [ ] Regional agencies and key staff
- [ ] Schools, colleges and universities
- [ ] Social and emergency services
- [ ] Special purpose authorities such as housing and transport
- [ ] Youth and senior citizens groups
- [ ] ....

See also 'Who to Involve' checklist in the *Toolbox* on **www.communityplanning.net**

Inviting involvement
Advertising hoarding and publicity leaflets

Team selection

Selecting the event 'Team' is one of the first tasks of the Team Chairperson and will shape the flavour of the entire event.

Team arrival
Event Team arriving by plane. The image of professionals 'flying in' to sort out problems is often criticised but bringing experience from other places can sometimes be valuable in stimulating fresh thinking. Having local Team members with long experience of the area can also work well, perhaps with an independent facilitator

PRINCIPLES

- Team size should reflect the scale and scope of the event. Usually 8–12 members works well.

- Team members should have a range of skills, interests and cultural backgrounds, tailored to the needs of the particular community and issues likely to be raised, preferably combined with facilitation and mediation skills.

- Team members should be free of any real or perceived conflicts of interest in the area, or if they have any interests these should be clearly stated.

- Team members should commit themselves to attending the entire event. (People unable to stay for the whole period should be Advisors instead.)

- Enlist the best professional expertise available within your area of influence.

"A heartfelt thank you to the government and councillors of Birmingham for inviting me to their city and so gracefully putting up with my comments. To ask people to come to see you and then allow them, encourage them even, to be frank in criticism as well as in praise is a sign of creative spirit."

Team member

TIPS

- Select people for what they know rather than who they are, and for their ability to analyse complex issues as part of a team. It is useful to have some people who have been Team members before.

- Give all Team members specific roles (see table right).

- Avoid people who are too similar. A balance of sexes and a range of ages is essential.

Team Roles and Responsibilities

Note: Several compatible roles may be taken by one individual

Title	Brief	Names
Team chairperson	Provide leadership, orchestrate event, take responsibility	....
Team facilitator	Keep roving eye on group dynamics, reporting back to Team Chairperson	....
Team coordinator	Logistics and overall organisation	....
Workshop facilitators	Facilitate workshops	....
Workshop note-takers	Prepare notes of workshops in format suitable for final report	....
Report editor	Commission and gather copy and illustrations. Prepare printer-ready layouts	....
Report subeditor	Subedit copy and assist editor	....
Report production	Oversee report production using desktop publishing software. Liaise with printer	....
Sound recorder	Record key sessions and index recordings	....
Diplomats	Liaise between different workshops to create linkages	....
Photographer	Ensure key events are photographed and images downloaded onto computer	....
Contacts person	Keep names and telephone numbers of useful resource people	....
Presentation editor	Compile presentation (usually in Powerpoint)	....
Stage manager	Coordinate pool of people for errands, etc	....
Follow-up coordinator	Ensure follow-up takes place and publicise	....

Skills Required

Team members should be good at analysing complex problems, be in good health, and be good at working with people. In addition each person should have skills in at least one, and preferably more than one, of the following:

☐ Urban design   ☐ Planning   ☐ Landscape design
☐ Property development   ☐ Economics and finance   ☐ Law
☐ Sociology   ☐ Management   ☐ Community development
☐ Architecture   ☐ Journalism   ☐ Ecology

Student support

To provide back-up for the event Team it is useful to have technical support before and during the event. Although volunteers or paid staff can provide this, it is often better to involve local students of architecture or related disciplines.

Help with logistics
Sorting workshop materials at a Community Planning Event

"It was like being back at college but I realised that there were 500 years of professional experience around the table. I came to the event as a cynic but left exhilarated. I have not had so much fun as a professional for some time. It recharged my batteries. When you hit the inevitable mid-life crisis in any project, having one of these events is a good way to give it a kick up the backside."

Mike Galloway
Regeneration Project
Director

PRINCIPLES

- Taking part in a Community Planning Event can be a rich learning experience in organisation, planning, architecture, participatory processes, research and presentation.

- Students can provide a creative and energetic labour force and will pass on process knowledge to others. Students of architecture, planning and urban design are generally most likely to benefit and be useful.

- Within an initial time framework set by their tutors, students should be directed by the Team Chair or other delegated Team member. Tutor interference during the event can cause serious difficulties.

TIPS

- Three or four students is enough to make a coherent workforce without dominating the event.

- Choose students who are energetic, keen, flexible, sociable, diplomatic and can take initiative. Wherever possible provide clear roles and briefs. Treat students as equal members of the creative effort, not dogsbodies.

- Encourage students to make a presentation of their experience afterwards.

Student Support Tasks

Before the event:

- ☐ Gather background material
- ☐ Generate publicity
- ☐ Get to know the site and local people
- ☐ Read this manual and other material
- ☐ Prepare exhibition and briefing for Team members
- ☐ Prepare base models and plans
- ☐ ....
- ☐ ....

Modelmaking
University students preparing a 3-metre-square model for a Community Planning Event. This became the focus for open-ended discussions with local people; problems and solutions being recorded on cards pinned to the model with cocktail sticks. A consensus view was thus established from which the design team could work

During the event:

- ☐ Maintain a library of information
- ☐ Service workshops
- ☐ Act as personal assistants to the Chairperson
- ☐ Take and collate photographs
- ☐ Participate in all activities as much as possible
- ☐ ....
- ☐ ....

After the event:

- ☐ Collate and store information for future use
- ☐ Monitor effectiveness of the event
- ☐ ....
- ☐ ....

Information gathering

It is important to provide enough information for participants both before and during an event, otherwise the event will be spent gathering information rather than thinking out the way forward.

PRINCIPLES

- Selecting and presenting information is a central element of the Community Planning Event process and should be directed by the Team Chairperson.

- A briefing pack should normally be sent out to the Team members (or all participants if by invitation only) two weeks beforehand. Other material can be placed on a website or made available at the event.

TIPS

- Use information that already exists where possible. Get key stakeholders to prepare presentations as this promotes active involvement.

- Start thinking about what will be needed for the final presentation and report right from the start. Collect data in the appropriate formats.

- Be selective. Too much information can overwhelm people and inhibit imaginative thinking.

- Set up a resource library and keep an index of useful material. Identify resource people to collect information on specific issues; eg jobs, history.

- Think visual. Good photos, drawings, maps and graphs are more useful than wordy reports.

- Tie important documents to table tops with string to avoid people mistaking them for handouts.

Briefing pack
Participants should get one before they arrive at an event so that there is time to digest it. Packs handed out on the day rarely get looked at

"The whole process was extremely creative. It brought a lot of people together."

Ted Watts
Past President
Royal Institute of
Chartered Surveyors

Basic Information Required

Not everything will be relevant on all occasions. Select what is and add anything else you think might be useful.

Maps, tables, reports, videos showing:
- ☐ Aerial photographs
- ☐ Blank base maps at various scales
- ☐ Concerns, constraints and opportunities lists
- ☐ Development plans and proposals, zoning and previous studies
- ☐ Employment patterns
- ☐ Historical data: archaeological, protected buildings, area development
- ☐ Information sources
- ☐ Land ownership, land availability and land valuation (including impact of over/under-supply in the future)
- ☐ Land use, transport and building condition
- ☐ Newspaper cuttings
- ☐ Planning context
- ☐ Political, administrative and cultural boundaries
- ☐ Political context
- ☐ Population statistics and projections
- ☐ Profiles of local organisations
- ☐ Social profiles
- ☐ Tax information
- ☐ Topography and ecology
- ☐ Tourist and area promotion information
- ☐ ....
- ☐ ....
- ☐ ....

Sample Briefing Pack Letter

Dear

Anytown Community Planning Event

Many thanks for agreeing to take part in this event as: [insert role, ie Team member, Advisor, Admin staff, student support].

A briefing pack is enclosed containing the following information for you to look at before you arrive:

- Mission statement
- Team list with roles and responsibilities
- Biographical notes on Team members
- Timetable
- Background material: (some of material listed in the Basic Information Required box left)
- List of what else will be available during the event
- *The Community Planning Event Manual*

Further background can be found on the following websites: [add URLs].

Accommodation and travel arrangements are as follows: [insert details with contact telephone numbers].

Payment and expenses arrangements are as follows: [insert details with any special restrictions on future commissions etc].

Please remember to bring your camera and any relevant photos or other material for the exhibition and presentation. Mark these clearly with your name if you want them returned. Bring digital files on a USB stick or CD in the following formats: [add details].

I would be grateful if you would confirm in writing that the above arrangements are satisfactory and look forward to seeing you at [place] on [date].

Yours sincerely

Team Chairperson

Publicity

Publicity is an essential aspect of a Community Planning Event in order to generate a public debate.

PRINCIPLES

- Publicity is needed:
  Before – to generate excitement and ensure participation;
  During – to maintain momentum and disseminate the results;
  After – to track progress and stimulate action.

- The local media should be involved as participants in the process as well as observers. It is a rare opportunity for the media to play a part in generating community solutions rather than simply reporting problems.

Media involvement
Community Planning Events can make stimulating television

"The public is eager for participation, elected councils are searching for new direction. Are Community Planning Events the missing ingredient?"

John Worthington
President
Urban Design Group

TIPS

- Time the event to coincide with a political opportunity or community event to provide added media attraction (but avoid major distractions, eg World Cup).

- Put one person in charge of media liaison as part of a general information headquarters.

- Maintain a comprehensive press kit explaining the issues and process. This can be the briefing pack (see page **33**) with the addition of press releases on special newsworthy issues.

- Try and get a special pull-out supplement in an established local newspaper. In addition produce a broadsheet including the programme.

- Hold a press conference prior to the event and show presentations of previous events. Invite the media to take part throughout but particularly for tours, briefings and presentations.

- T-shirts, badges and banners can all be useful.

- Encourage local organisations to help with publicity by, for instance, writing letters to the local paper or leafleting in lively public places.

- Maintain a clippings file of press coverage.

Creating a public debate
Publicising the future of people's environment is an essential part of Community Planning Events

Venues

On location
Marquees can be used for workshop sessions and exhibitions where no large halls are available on site

"Community Planning Events can change the way we plan because you focus on the area, you are in the area when you focus on it and you involve the people with a particular interest in seeing the area come to life. Normally you would be in an office framework, divorced from the site, and not in contact with the community that will be living in the environment that you create."

**Charmaine Young
Housing Developer**

Premises which provide a stimulating atmosphere are essential. Four main types of space are required:

PRINCIPLES

- **Large hall** for public meetings, presentations and exhibitions with toilets and refreshment facilities.

- **Medium-sized rooms** for workshops, group meetings and a crèche.

- **Studio workspace** for the Team and organisers with lockable administration room, kitchen and toilets. 24-hour access essential.

- **Living accommodation** for Team members and organisers (for longer events).

Ideally these should be next to one another and within, or close by, the area being studied to make it easier for people to keep focussed on the task in hand.

TIPS

- Prominent venues on 'neutral ground' work best. Vacant shopfronts and schools can be ideal. Check venues are available for the whole period.

- It helps if all Team members and other key participants stay in the same place, preferably a good hotel with individual rooms (as people may need to sleep at different times). Late night bar and breakfast discussions can be very productive. Accommodation within easy walking distance will avoid endless logistic problems.

- Quiet outdoor space can be useful for workshops in warm weather.

Making do
Six workshops in a fairly confined space is tolerable because the room is carpeted which muffles the sound

Good Room Arrangement

Room layout one might aim at if specifying in the abstract. In practice one has to improvise with spaces available.

Flexible space
Six workshops taking place simultaneously in a large hall. The same space was used for public meetings, presentations and Team working

workshop	screens	crèche		editing
workshop	large hall	kitchen / wc	studio	
workshop	exhibition	reception		administration

Fittings and services

The venues need to be properly equipped and serviced if the event is to function smoothly.

Room services
Conference room set up for workshops (above); using the built-in facilities of a local authority council chamber (below)

"The community planning weekends were brilliant. People could really get to talk to somebody and get a straight answer. There was a nice atmosphere."

**Joan Maginn
Residents' Association
Chair**

PRINCIPLES

- All work and domestic needs of the participants should be met for the duration of the event. People should be able to arrive empty-handed and operate as efficiently, if not more so, than if they were in their own workplaces.

- Venues should be set up well before the public arrives and Team members will normally help with this.

TIPS

- Self-service catering with a constant supply of hot drinks and nibbles works well, so that people do not feel bound by fixed breaks. Dinner can usefully be more formal to provide a change of pace.

- Rapid photocopier and computer repair service is essential. If in doubt have spare machines.

- Make sure heating systems can be made to remain on overnight.

Fittings

Checklist for large-scale 5-day event with a Team of 12. Adjust for smaller events.

Studio Workspace

- [ ] Chairs (office) and stools
- [ ] Computers (see page **43**)
- [ ] Desks for writing (4), computers (10) and drawing (3)
- [ ] Drawing boards or drawing tables (8)
- [ ] Drinks facility and fridge
- [ ] Lighting, including desk lighting
- [ ] Lock-up for valuable equipment
- [ ] Pin board or pin-up wall
- [ ] Photocopier (see page **43**)
- [ ] Plan and drawing storage system
- [ ] Power outlets
- [ ] Shelving and filing space
- [ ] Table (conference) with seats for 16
- [ ] Telephones and fax
- [ ] Waste bins and garbage bags
- [ ] ....

Large Hall

- [ ] Blackout curtains
- [ ] Chairs – movable
- [ ] Disability access
- [ ] Exhibition facilities
- [ ] Flipchart (with non-squeaky pens)
- [ ] Induction loop
- [ ] Lighting (friendly)
- [ ] Lock-up area for valuables
- [ ] Projection screens (2 large)
- [ ] Public address system with microphones on stands and roving
- [ ] Tables for breakout work
- [ ] ....

Medium-sized rooms

- [ ] Chairs – movable
- [ ] Flipcharts
- [ ] Pin board and pin-up space
- [ ] Table
- [ ] ....

Services

Checklist for large-scale event. Adjust accordingly.

- [ ] Caretaking/reception to provide security for equipment: 24-hour
- [ ] Catering: breakfast at hotel, buffet lunches, set dinners in a variety of venues, constant supply of hot and cold drinks, fruit and nibbles
- [ ] Computer support (rapid, 24-hour cover on final night)
- [ ] Internet access
- [ ] Photocopier repair service: rapid, 24-hour cover
- [ ] Printers: briefed well in advance of scope of work and importance of deadlines
- [ ] Telephone lines: two minimum
- [ ] Transport: bikes, minibuses or coaches for Team tours and travel to evening dinner venues
- [ ] ....
- [ ] ....
- [ ] ....

Back room services
Space and services for the organisers nearby

Equipment and supplies

A substantial amount of equipment is required to run a Community Planning Event successfully.

- Support bodies may well have much of the equipment. Otherwise it will have to be borrowed, hired or bought.

- Equipment and supplies should be organised well in advance (see checklist on next spread).

- It is better to over-provide than run out. Arrangements should allow for returning or reusing any surpluses.

- Discourage mobile phones in the working sessions but they can be useful for dealing with press enquiries, suppliers and emergencies.

- Agree and standardise computer software. Prepare standard layout formats beforehand.

- Banners for the entrance, the main hall and workshops can usefully be prepared in advance.

Team Members' Luggage

- ☐ Smartish clothes for the start and finish
- ☐ Casual clothes for the working sessions
- ☐ Camera
- ☐ Useful general facts and figures or illustrative material likely to be relevant
- ☐ Material for special presentation if required
- ☐ Any special favourite drawing pens
- ☐ ....
- ☐ ....
- ☐ ....

"A successful event has to be as carefully stage managed as a theatre production – but one in which the audience and actors keep reversing roles."

**Debbie Radcliffe
Actress and Team member**

Stationery
Supplies laid out at the start of a workshop. Never risk running out. Surpluses can always be made use of later if you can stop people walking off with it

Pretty colours
Using Post-it notes in several colours. Visually it looks more interesting and different colours can be used to denote different categories or priorities

Equipment and Supplies

Checklist for large-scale event. Adjust accordingly.

A ESSENTIAL ITEMS
for most events

☐ Aerial photographs
☐ Banners and directional signs with fixings
☐ Base maps and plans of the area at different scales (1:200 and 1:400 most commonly used)
☐ Blu-tak
☐ Camera: 35mm or digital with wide-angle, telephoto, flash and close-up facility
☐ Camera: Polaroid (for last-minute shots)
☐ Camera accessories (for digital): memory cards, battery charger, spare battery, connection cable, card reader, download cable
☐ Clipboards
☐ Crayons for children to draw with
☐ Data projector and screen
☐ Extension cables
☐ Flipcharts (with non-squeaky pens)
☐ Layout pads (grid marked with non-repro blue ink)
☐ Mobile phones, including rechargers
☐ Name badges (and/or blank sticky labels)
☐ Paper: tracing paper rolls; A5 note pads; flipchart pads; A4 plain
☐ Pens: felt-tips in bright colours and grey tones (different sizes); fibre-tipped with medium and fine tips (black and red); ball points (black and red); technical drawing (1 set); highlighters (in different colours); marker pens (in different colours)
☐ Pins (different colours): drawing pins; safety pins; stickpins
☐ Pointer stick/laser pointer for presentations
☐ Post-its (different sizes and at least 4 colours)
☐ Pritt-stick glue
☐ Rubber bands
☐ Rubbish bags
☐ Rulers and scale rulers
☐ Scissors
☐ Signing-in sheets
☐ Spray mount adhesive
☐ Tape: brown packaging tape; double sided; heavy duty (for outdoor use)/gaffer; magic; masking; clear rolls (sellotape)
☐ USB stick
☐ Velcro pads (sticky hook and loop pads)
☐ Zip-up bags (for Hands-on Planning kits)
☐ ....
☐ ....

B POSSIBLY USEFUL ITEMS
especially for lengthy events

☐ Base model with movable parts
☐ Box files
☐ Cardboard or polystyrene (for model making)
☐ Clock with alarm (for timing speakers)
☐ Cocktail sticks (for use with model)
☐ Coloured sticky dots (red, green, yellow)
☐ Crayons and paper for children
☐ Cutting knives, mats, metal edge and spare blades

- [ ] Exhibition facilities
- [ ] Overhead or opaque projectors with transparency film and markers (handy for sketching and for presentations)
- [ ] Paper clips
- [ ] Pin board or pin-up wall
- [ ] Public address system with microphones on stands and roving, plus induction loop
- [ ] Scalpels and blades
- [ ] Video camera and accessories
- [ ] Video playback equipment
- [ ] ....
- [ ] ....

C TEAM WORKING ITEMS
where full office capacity is required

- [ ] Calculator
- [ ] Computer equipment:
  - [ ] Colour printer and toner
  - [ ] Laptops
  - [ ] Mobile server, hub and connections
  - [ ] Scanner
  - [ ] Screen wipes
  - [ ] Software: word processing; desktop publishing (DTP); computer aided design (CAD); Photoshop. Other as specified by Team members
    - [ ] CDs, PC and Mac compatible
- [ ] Correction fluid
- [ ] Fax machine
- [ ] Pads (24"x 30")
- [ ] Erasers
- [ ] Hole puncher
- [ ] Layout pads (grid marked with non-repro blue ink)
- [ ] Paper:
  A4, A3 & A2 sketch pads
  A4 writing pads (lined)
- [ ] Paperclips

- [ ] Paper trimmer or guillotine
- [ ] Pencils: normal; coloured
- [ ] Photocopier paper, toner etc
- [ ] Ring binders (A4 and A3 with plastic pockets to protect drawings)
- [ ] Stapler and staple extractors
- [ ] T-squares, triangles and circle templates
- [ ] ....
- [ ] ....

D VENUE ITEMS
if not provided (see also *Fittings and services* page **38**)

- [ ] Blackout curtains
- [ ] Catering gear (cups, plates, cutlery, napkins, urn, kettle, etc)
- [ ] Cleaning fluid
- [ ] Chairs (stackable?) and stools
- [ ] Fridge and/or cold drinks facility
- [ ] Flipcharts (with non-squeaky pens)
- [ ] Food and drink
- [ ] Lock-up for valuable equipment
- [ ] Photocopier with enlarging/reducing facility (with rapid repair service)
- [ ] Projector stand
- [ ] Sanitary equipment if venue on abandoned site, including laminated toilet signs
- [ ] Lighting / spotlighting to improve poorly lit room
- [ ] Tables / desks (for Hands-on Planning)
- [ ] Waste bins and rubbish bags
- [ ] ....
- [ ] ....

See also 'Equipment and supplies' checklist in the *Toolbox* on **www.communityplanning.net**

Computers and information technology

Making the most of recent advances in information technology can make Community Planning Events much easier to organise and more effective.

PRINCIPLES

- Establishing a project website or having space on an existing site is a highly cost-effective way of making project information available before an event and making the results available afterwards (but should not be relied on exclusively).

- Use of digital cameras, desktop publishing (DTP) software and Powerpoint presentations makes it easy to communicate visually – essential for planning and design issues – and to keep records.

- Use of editing facilities in word processing and DTP software, combined with email, enables participatory editing of documents by stakeholders with relative ease.

- Portable hardware can be used to establish a fully functioning design and editing office in any location.

TIPS

- Powerpoint presentations can be left with clients afterwards, enabling them to present to others.

- Use event reports as a way of packaging all useful information about a project for future reference.

- Identify technicians familiar with all hardware and software who can be available at short notice during an event to resolve any problems.

- Make sure all computer equipment is compatible.

- Establish templates for documents beforehand.

Useful software

Checklist for large scale event. Adjust accordingly.

- ☐ Microsoft Office (Word, Powerpoint and Excel)
- ☐ DTP (desktop publishing)
- ☐ CAD (computer aided design)
- ☐ Adobe Acrobat Professional for editing and participatory editing of pdf documents.
- ☐ ....
  ....

"Nothing is random. Logistics and computer organisation are essential. Everything is organised to satisfy people's material needs. Only their thinking matters."

**Eléonore Hauptmann
Urban planner, France
Chairman, DIALOG**

Fully functioning editing and design office
Widespread availability of laptops makes it possible for Team members to be as productive as if in their own offices

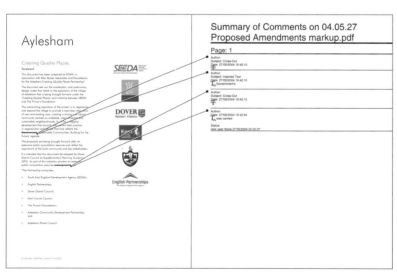

Participatory editing
Screen shot of proposed changes to a draft report using Acrobat software which allows comments on graphics as well as text

People's visions
A local resident presents her ideas for the future of her community at a Community Planning Event

Section 4
The event

Timetabling

Launch
*Sample leaflet for
circulation before an event*

*"The participation of
citizens in almost every
aspect of the process is its
key to success. The process
provides a structured
approach through which
citizens, politicians and
professionals can speak and
listen to each others'
concerns and ideas and
raise the consciousness of
the community."*

**American Institute
of Architects**

Skilful and imaginative timetabling is the key to
organising successful Community Planning Events.

PRINCIPLES

- The length of an event should be determined by the
  complexity of the issues and the resources available
  but the structure will be similar in most cases.
  Longer events often span a weekend to allow both
  professionals and locals to get easily involved.

- Events are made up of a series of presentations,
  workshops, visits, public meetings, working sessions
  and social events. Some of these will be open to
  everyone, others will be for specific groups only.

- The timetable should be determined and circulated
  well in advance so that people can fix it in their
  diaries and prepare themselves.

- Sample timetables for a range of common event
  types are on the next few pages. See also the
  sample timetables in the *Toolbox* on
  www.communityplanning.net

TIPS

- Short events – 1 or 2 days – are useful for relatively
  simple issues or small areas but do not expect to be
  able to deal with all of the problems of a city or
  neighbourhood in that time. Events lasting 4 or 5
  days are usually necessary for people to learn to
  work together and think through the issues.

- Do not let the timetable inhibit spontaneity. The
  Chairperson should allow some 'unstructuring' and
  flexibility if it seems appropriate.

- Allow time for relaxed meals; both buffet and
  sit-down. They are a good opportunity for speakers
  and for discussion.

- Allow time for Team discussion on process; ie 'how to work as a team'. Encourage people to share their 'learning moments'.

- Keep people healthy by encouraging walking, swimming, and so on, preferably in groups. An intensive pace is essential but pushing people too hard can be counterproductive.

Timetable Structure

Note the common format regardless of length. Adjust to suit circumstances.

		5-Day Event		1-Day Event
INTRODUCTION	Thursday	Tour of area for Team members Briefings from key players Launch event	**Morning Session 1**	Introductions Briefings from key players Coffee
PROBLEMS/ OPPORTUNITIES	Friday	Open topic-based workshops to identify key problems and opportunities	**Morning Session 2**	Discussion/analysis of key problems and opportunities Lunch
SOLUTIONS/ OPTIONS	Saturday	Open design workshops to explore future options Team brainstorm over dinner	**Afternoon Session 1**	Design sessions to explore future options Tea
SYNTHESIS/ ANALYSIS	Sunday	Team analysis and determination of strategy Report writing and drawing	**Afternoon Session 2**	Drafting of notes on conclusions and next steps
PRODUCTION/ PRESENTATION	Monday	Produce report and presentation Present conclusions at public meeting or open house	**Afterwards** **Few days later**	Production and distribution of report Public meeting or open house

Sample timetables for some event types

PROCESS

12.40	POST IT BRAINSTORM
12.50	OUTSIDERS POST & TALK
1.00	INSIDERS POST & TALK
13.10	SELECT THEMES & TEAMS
13.20	DEVELOP PROPOSALS
14.00	REPORT BACK BY TEAMS
14.15	BREAK
14.30	PREPARE PRESENTATIONS
3.15	LEAVE

Good manners
*Letting people know what
they are doing when.
Workshop timetable on a
flipchart at a Community
Planning Event*

*"Exciting … innovative …
we hadn't conceived when
we came into the beginning
of this week as to how it
might have finished …
what has been proposed so
far is radically different
from the outline, and this
just reflects the wide variety
of personnel that has been
brought together on this
exercise."*

**Don Chroston
Design Champion
Mental Health NHS Trust**

Every event will be unique and have a unique timetable but a number of different event types have emerged which are most clearly identifiable by their timetables.

PRINCIPLES

- The timetable – a detailed breakdown of what happens when – is the key tool for understanding how Community Planning Events work in practice and how one event differs from another.

- The sample timetables on the following pages are based on real events that have happened and been successful. They show the sequence and timing of activities as well as who is invited, or expected, to attend each activity.

- Sample timetables should only be used as a starting point for planning events, not as blueprints. The logic and logistics of each event should be thought through carefully by event organisers.

TIPS

- Timetables with the level of detail shown here are for organisers, and perhaps Team members. Simplified ones will be more useful for others.

- Displaying timetables on a flipchart or wallchart is sometimes better than printing them on paper, providing you can rely on people to attend in the first place.

- When someone proposes an event always ask to see a timetable. The same event type can be given different names, and events with the same name can vary considerably.

Event Types

Overview of the event types with sample timetables shown on the following pages. By no means a comprehensive listing. Selection made to illustrate some popular approaches and the scope for ingenuity. For more types, to suggest new ones and to download editable templates see the *Toolbox* on **www.communityplanning.net**

	Characteristics	Main strengths
Collaborative Design Workshop	• Open house evening • 1-day workshop • Report back evening	Enabling the public to make an input into proposals already part developed by professionals
Community Planning Weekend	• 5-day event spanning Weekend • Local hosts, professional team • Specific public sessions	Involving local communities in developing major neighbourhood regeneration and development proposals
Enquiry by Design	• 4-day event during the week • Led by multidisciplinary design team • Stakeholder and public sessions	Masterplanning for new build or regeneration, especially where new design thinking is required
Reinvigorate	• 1-day event on a weekday • Local stakeholders and outsiders • Facilitation team	Stimulating informed debate and action on a local issue of wider generic interest
Stakeholder Participation Day	• 1-day event on a Saturday • Participants invited in advance	Initial engagement of all stakeholders in the development of planning policies

Sample timetable **Collaborative Design Workshop**

- 3-stage event
- Open house evening
- 1-day workshop for key stakeholders
- Report back evening

DAY 1 TUESDAY
OPEN HOUSE

14.00	**Setting up** Room arrangements. Delivery of equipment and supplies. Erection of banners and signs
18.00	**Review** arrangements
19.00	**Arrivals** Review exhibition, refreshments
19.30	**Introduction & briefing** By organisers and experts
20.00	**Open house** Interactive displays, questionnaires, networking
21.30	**Close**

Interim period – several days

Analysis By organisers. Review of open house results. Preparation for key stakeholder workshop

DAY 2 FRIDAY
STAKEHOLDER WORKSHOP

8.30	**Set up** By organisers and facilitators
9.00	**Registration, Coffee and exhibition viewing**
9.30	**Welcome** By organisers or politician and facilitators
9.45	**Briefings** By politicians, officials and consultants
10.40	**Coffee break**
10.55	**Key issues workshops** Discussion in groups
11.25	**Key issues plenary** Report back from groups
12.00	**Site reconnaissance** Walk or coach tour

Origins

The Collaborative Design Workshop approach was first developed by English Partnerships in 2004 for its Heart of East Greenwich project, London.

Main Uses

Enabling the public to make an input into proposals already part developed by professionals.

Organisers includes at least one facilitator
and key design team members

Attendance

DAY 2 contd

DAY 3 MONDAY
REPORT BACK

13.00	**Lunch and exhibition viewing**	
14.00	**Design workshops** Working in groups	
15.30	**Tea break**	
16.00	**Design plenary** Report back from groups	
17.00	**Next steps** Statement by organisers. Brief discussion perhaps	
17.30	**Event close** Refreshments and networking (optional)	

Interim period – several days

Analysis
By organisers. Review of workshop results. Preparation for report back presentation

16.00	**Setting up** Room arrangements Erection of additional displays	
18.00	**Review** arrangements	
19.00	**Arrivals** Review exhibition	
19.30	**Presentation** By organisers and experts	
20.30	**Debate** Questions and discussion	
21.00	**Networking** Exhibition viewing & feedback. Refreshments	
21.30	**Close**	

Interim period – several days

Event report and record
Circulation by organisers.
Paper and web versions

Common Variations

The amount of time between the three stages can be varied to suit the capacity of the organisers to analyse and present the material produced. The less time the better to maintain public interest and project momentum.

Further Information

Case Studies on **www.communityplanning.net**
(Heart of East Greenwich)

Sample timetable **Community Planning Weekend**

- 5-day event spanning weekend
- Local hosts, professional team
- Specific public sessions

DAY 1 THURSDAY
BRIEFING

08.00	**Setting up** Room arrangements. Delivery of equipment and supplies. Erection of banners and signs
12.00	**Team assembles**
13.00	**Buffet lunch** Welcome by hosts, sponsors etc
14.00	**Reconnaissance** By team of area by bus/train/plane/foot
16.00	**Political briefings** By local politicians
17.00	**Community briefings** By local inhabitants
18.00	**Technical briefings** By planners, engineers, developers etc
19.00	**Team briefing** By Chairperson on Team working processes
19.30	**Launch event** (optional) Public meeting and/or dinner/reception

DAY 2 FRIDAY
ISSUES

09.00	**Team briefing and preparation**
10.00	**Setting the scene** Presentations by local interests
11.00	**Topic workshops** Open to all, punctuated by lunch and tea breaks. Several parallel topic-based groups ending with plenary report back (or one single open plenary workshop).
17.00	**Team review** Detailed problem definition
18.00	**Breather** Minute writing, reading, exercise
20.00	**Team dinner**

DAY 3 SATURDAY
SOLUTIONS

09.00	**Team briefing and preparation**
10.00	**Report back on Day 2** By Chairperson and/or Team members
10.30	**Lessons from elsewhere** Presentations by Team members

Common Variations

- **1 day shorter or longer** The American Institute of Architects favours a slightly shorter 4-day event which can be more suitable for busy Team members: Team arrives Thursday evening. Reconnaissance and briefing on Friday morning. 6-day events have become popular in the UK with the final presentation on Tuesday.

- **Delayed presentation** The final presentation can be delayed for a few days. But having longer to prepare has to be weighed against the loss of momentum and some participants.

- **Delayed report** A popular option is to produce a broadsheet with a summary for the final presentation and for a small editorial team to complete the report over the next few days.

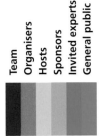

Team Organisers Hosts Sponsors Invited experts General public

People may attend more sessions than indicated subject to approval by the Team Chair

Attendance

DAY 3 contd

12.00	**Design workshops** Open to all, punctuated by lunch and tea breaks and ending with a plenary report back. In parallel groups of 10–15
17.00	**Team review** Developing central themes
18.00	**Breather** Minute writing, reading, exercise
19.00	**Team brainstorm dinner** Imaginative solutions

DAY 4 SUNDAY TEAM WORKING

10.00	**Team preparation**
11.00	**Team editorial meeting** Report, presentation and production structure
12.00	**Report and presentation production** Writing, editing, drawing, Powerpoint show. Review meetings as necessary. Team only. Sleep and eat as and when

Origins

The Community Planning Weekend approach (illustrated here) was refined by John Thompson & Partners as a key component of its consultancy services. The practice facilitated more than 50 Community Planning Weekends between 1989 and 2008.

DAY 5 MONDAY PRESENTATION

07.00	**Printers deadline** Report and/or broadsheet to printers
All day	**Presentation preparation** Image and text selection. Exhibition mounting. Hall arrangements
All day	**Clearing up** Tidying up, packing equipment and supplies
17.30	**Press briefing**
19.00	**Public presentation** Powerpoint show followed by discussion and formal thanks. Distribution of report or broadsheet
21.00	**Farewell social event**

Main Uses

Involving local communities in developing major neighbourhood regeneration and development proposals.

Further Information

- John Thompson & Partners (see *Contacts*, page **94**)

- *Case Studies* on **www.communityplanning.net** (Caterham Barracks Village; Lübeck)

Sample timetable **Enquiry by Design (EbD)**

- 4-day event during the week
- Led by multidisciplinary design team
- Stakeholder and public sessions

DAY 1 TUESDAY: SETTING SCENE

9.00	**Setting up** By core team and key stakeholders
9.15	**Registration**
9.30	**Welcome and introduction** Process so far, event purpose
9.45	**Stakeholder statements** Short presentations on each organisation's background and visions
10.30	**Presentations on principles** eg Sustainability and local urbanism
11.30	**Technical briefings** eg planning constraints
12.00	**Lunch**
13.00	**Design session 1** Analysis. In groups dealing with: community facilities; neighbourhood analysis; transport and movement; landscape and sustainability.
16.00	**Conclusions of Day 1** Plenary session
17.00	**Break**

DAY 1 contd

18.30	**Open house session** Presentation on EbD process. Opportunity for general public to meet informally with design team and make comments on exhibits.
20.30	**Close**

DAY 2 WEDNESDAY EXPLORING ISSUES

9.00	**Aims of the day** Presentation on Day 1. Aims and structure of Day 2
9.30	**Design session 2** Specialised groups focus on: masterplan; regeneration; landscape; transport; land use
12.00	**Lunch**
13.00	**Design session 2** (cont)
15.30	**Break**
16.00	**Feedback plenary** Initial concept plan
17.30	**Close**

Core design team
Key stakeholders
Expert stakeholders
Wider stakeholders
General public

Attendance

Stakeholder categories

Key stakeholders = parties most affected eg landowners, local authorities, local community
Expert stakeholders = representitives of stakeholders with specialist technical or general knowledge eg a local authority planner, a consultant geologist
Wider stakeholders = parties affected to a lesser degree eg neighbouring parish, regional NGO

DAY 3 THURSDAY: CONCEPTS

9.00	**Aims of the day** Presentation on Days 1 & 2. Aims and structure of Day 3. Questions and answers
9.30	**Design session 3** Developing initial concepts In groups
13.00	**Lunch**
13.30	**Design session 3** (cont)
16.00	**Team feedback plenary**
17.30	**Open session** For stakeholders to view progress and make comments
19.00	**Close**

DAY 4 FRIDAY
FINAL OUTPUTS

9.00	**Aims of the day**
9.30	**Questions and answers**
10.00	**Design session 4** Refining concepts. In groups
13.00	**Lunch**

DAY 4 contd

13.45	**Production and preparation** Final drawings and strategies
19.00	**Public presentation** Team presentation, discussion, feedback
21.30	**Close**

Origins
The Enquiry by Design (EbD) approach was developed by The Prince's Foundation, London. Some 12 EbD Events were organised between 1999 and 2008. The term Enquiry by Design has been trademarked by the Foundation with English Partnerships.

Main Uses
Masterplanning for new build and regeneration especially where new design thinking is required.

Common Variations
- **Split event** The process can be split up into separate events held a few weeks apart. This allows time for background teamwork but can lead to loss of momentum and more costs.

Further Information
- The Prince's Foundation (see *Contacts,* page **94**)
- *Case Studies* on **www.communityplanning.net** (Aylesham) and **www.princes-foundation.org** (projects and practice)
- *Sustainable Urban Extensions: Planned through Design* (see *Publications and sources,* page **92**)

Sample timetable **Reinvigorate**

- 1-day event on a weekday
- Local stakeholders and outsiders
- Facilitation team

DAY 1 MONDAY: SET UP

16.00 **Setting up**
Venue arrangements. Delivery of equipment and supplies. Erection of banners and signs

17.00 **Facilitator briefing**
For organisers and facilitators. Run through process. Check venues and transport

19.00 **Dinner**
For organisers and facilitators

DAY 2 TUESDAY: THE EVENT

8.30 **Set up**
By organisers and facilitators

10:00 **Registration & coffee**
At main venue (central location). Hand out briefing packs

10.15 **Welcome**
Introduction by organiser. Presentation on relevant generic topic eg Mixed and balanced communities

DAY 2 contd

10.45 **Reconnaissance**
Brief guided tours of region (normally by coach) ending at local neighbourhood venues (one or more depending on number of participants)

12.00 **Workshop introduction**
Local briefings at each of the venues, explanation of the afternoon task

12.15 **Key challenges and opportunities**
1. First impressions – from the outsiders (Post-its and sort into groups)
2. Local knowledge – reality check from insiders (Post-its and sort into groups)
3. Set teams and themes

13.00 **Working lunch**
Work collaboratively around tables to generate Reinvigorating ideas. Prepare presentations

15.30 **Return to main venue**

Local stakeholders
Ousiders
Facilitators
Local & national organisers

Outsiders = Professionals and non-professionals from elsewhere who attend a reinvigorate event as a learning experience, in the same way as they might attend a conference.

Attendance

DAY 2 contd

16.15 **Panel introductions**
Panel members – key stakeholders

16.30 **Report backs**
From each neigbourhood

17.10 **Panel responses and pledges**

17.30 **Reception**
Networking

Interim period – several days

Event report
Produced and circulated by national or local organisers

Interim period – several weeks

Review session
For organisers and local stakeholders to plan next steps

Origins

The Reinvigorate approach was developed by the British Urban Regeneration Association (BURA). Four pilot Reinvigorate Events were organised in 2006 and 2007.

Main uses

Stimulating informed debate and action on a local issue of wider generic interest.

Variations

Participants can all take part in the same workshop or split into several. This will depend on the nature of the generic topic and the number of participants signing up.

Warning

The success of the Reinvigorate formula in achieving results on the ground has not been adequately evaluated as yet. The approach is included here to demonstrate the range of timetable possibilities.

Further Information

- British Urban Regeneration Association (BURA) (see *Contacts,* page **94**)

- *Case Studies* on **www.communityplanning.net** (Bristol)

Sample timetable **Stakeholder Participation Day**

- 1-day event (on a Saturday)
- Participants – cross section of key stakeholders – invited in advance
- Independent facilitator

DAY 1 FRIDAY SETUP

16.00	**Setting up** Room arrangements. Delivery of equipment and supplies. Erection of banners and signs
17.00	**Facilitator's briefing** For organisers and workshop leaders. Run through process
19.00	**Dinner** For organisers and facilitators

DAY 2 SATURDAY THE EVENT

8.30	**Set up** By organisers and facilitators
9.00	**Registration, coffee and exhibition viewing**
9.30	**Welcome** By organisers or politician and facilitators
9.45	**Briefings** By politicians, officials, and consultants
10.40	**Coffee break**

DAY 2 contd

10.55	**Key issues workshops** Discussion in groups
11.25	**Key issues plenary** Report back from groups
12.00	**Site reconnaissance** Walk or coach tour
13.00	**Lunch and exhibition viewing**
14.00	**Design workshops** Working in groups
15.30	**Tea break**
16.00	**Design plenary** Report back from groups
17.00	**Next steps** Statement by organisers. Brief discussion perhaps
17.30	**Event close** Refreshments and networking (optional)
18.00	**Clear up and review** By facilitators and organisers

	Event report Produced and circulated as soon as possible

Attendance

Origins

The Stakeholder Participation Day approach was developed by Cambridge City Council in 2003 for producing an Area Development Framework for part of the City. The same formula was repeated for another part of the city one year later.

Main Uses

Initial engagement of all stakeholders in the development of planning policies.

Common Variations

- **Reconnaissance earlier** The day can start with a reconnaissance or it can be omitted altogether (not recommended).

- **Public presentation** A presentation or open house event can be held in the evening to present the day's findings to the general public and/or the media and/or key stakeholders unable to attend. Alternatively this could be delayed to coincide with publication of the event report.

Further Information

- See Cambridge Southern Fringe, 2003, page **100**

Briefing

Community Planning Events start with activities designed to provide the participants with a comprehensive overview of the locality and issues being dealt with. These normally include a physical reconnaissance and a series of short presentations.

Briefing presentation
An architect sets the scene

"The event was a superb opportunity for me to step out of my comfort zone and tackle challenges with which I don't usually engage (eg physical regeneration). It was great to work with a multi-disciplinary team on a real issue."

Participant
Reinvigorate event

PRINCIPLES

- Presentations are made by all the main players so that the participants gain a rounded perspective; eg politicians of different persuasions, community groups, planners, landowners.

- Locals take part as guides on the reconnaissance but the Team Chairperson should direct it to avoid it becoming a public relations exercise for sectional interests.

TIPS

- Presentations should be short sharp overviews. Don't let people waffle on and monopolise the time.

- Some people may prefer to say a few words during a meal break rather than in a formal meeting and this provides variety and interest.

- Record presentations for later use. Keep names and phone numbers of contacts who may be helpful.

- Viewing from a hill, high tower or helicopter/light plane is particularly useful (although costly compared with obtaining aerial photos).

- Ask everyone to wear name badges and introduce themselves when they first speak.

Reconnaissance
Viewing from the air, from an open top bus and on foot

Topic workshops

Topic workshops, also known as 'briefing' workshops, are a way of creating a relaxed environment for exchanging information and identifying key issues. They usually take place in the early stages after the briefings.

Individual input
Participants each write their thoughts down on Post-it notes or cards

"It was one of the very few occasions when you had the opportunity to see all the people who would be involved in something like that at the same place at the same time, and actually discussing things without discussing them behind closed doors in small groups. So it was a far more open process than you would get in any normal circumstance."

**John Barnard
Residents Association
Acting Chairperson**

PRINCIPLES

- Participants are allocated to (or choose) a workshop. Each workshop will normally deal with a different topic; eg housing, transport, ecology. Team members are distributed evenly according to their expertise. Groups may vary in size, but 10–12 is a good number to aim at.

- Each workshop needs a facilitator, note-taker, mapper (who marks points on a map or plan) and storyboarder (who summarises key points on a flipchart). Roles can be amalgamated if necessary.

- Each workshop explores the issues allocated to it and prepares a presentation summarising its conclusions.

TIPS

- There are many ways of running workshops. One way to start is to ask everyone to write on Post-it notes, 3 things right and 3 things wrong with the present situation. Then categorise and review.

- Simple rules (eg no personal criticism) can be useful and should be displayed. Encourage experts to take a back seat and initially let locals take the lead.

- Write up reports immediately to inform the next link in the chain. Use bullet points under standard headings: 'who attended'; 'main issues'; 'proposals'.

- Keep attendance lists for reference later.

Sample Workshop Brief

Topic area: eg 'Housing 'or 'Transport'
1. What's wrong with existing situation?
2. What's right with existing situation?
3. What do we want (best hopes)?
4. How do we get there?

Topic Workshop Props

- [ ] Attendance sheets (name, address, organisation if any)
- [ ] Banner with workshop title
- [ ] Felt-tip pens (for storyboarding)
- [ ] Flipchart
- [ ] Large maps, aerial photos, etc
- [ ] Notepads
- [ ] Pens or pencils (for all participants)
- [ ] Pin-up area
- [ ] Post-its (4 different colours)
- [ ] Rules (if any)
- [ ] Standard report form
- [ ] Tape, Velcro, pins, Blu-tak
- [ ] Workshop brief

Joint output
Groups discuss and prioritise points made by individuals and draw conclusions and recommendations for reporting to the next plenary session

Facilitation Tips

- [ ] Introduce yourself and get others to do likewise
- [ ] Introduce session format. Ensure everyone understands task in hand
- [ ] Steer discussion to ensure progress
- [ ] Ensure everyone has chance to speak
- [ ] Deal with any conflict
- [ ] End with conclusions and next steps
- [ ] Agree a heading for the group's work
- [ ] Agree who will report the group's results to the plenary session (may be a team effort)

Opening plenary workshop

An opening plenary workshop involving everyone present is an alternative way of identifying key issues at the start of an event.*

"The basic notion is to get ideas which come out of the community's guts rather than ones which are imposed on them by remote authorities."

**Patrick Harrison
Secretary
Royal Institute of
British Architects**

* This method was pioneered by John Thompson & Partners, and is used at the beginning of all community planning weekends

PRINCIPLES

- Participants are seated theatre style in a semicircle facing three display sheets with suitable headings, eg 'problems', 'dreams', 'solutions'.

- Following introductory remarks on the purpose of the exercise, the organisers or facilitators ask participants to write any perceived 'problems' on Post-it notes. These are collected and read out before being posted on the 'problem' sheet. Any debate generated is recorded on a flipchart.

- The process is repeated for 'dreams' and 'solutions'.

- The anonymity of the process enables everyone to have an equal say and prevents over-domination by outspoken individuals.

TIPS

- This process is likely to bring out any negativity or conflict between participants and organisers at the outset and requires experienced facilitation.

- One, preferably two, facilitators need to focus entirely on facilitating the debate. Several assistant facilitators are needed to hand out and collect Post-it notes, group and categorise them on the boards and flipchart the debate.

- Photographs to record the proceedings should be taken throughout.

Team facilitation

Facilitator 1 stimulates debate by reading out Post-it notes. Facilitator 2 takes a microphone to anyone who wants to speak and collects more Post-its. Facilitator 3 sorts Post-its into categories on a wall chart. Facilitator 4 records the debate on a flipchart

Design workshops

Design workshops provide a 'hands-on' technique for allowing groups of people to work together creatively on physical planning and design. Sometimes called 'Hands-on Planning' sessions, they normally take place after the main issues have been identified.

The more the merrier
Any number of people can take part if there are enough tables and chairs

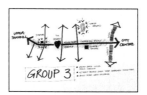

Output
Summary drawing of one workshop's proposals

"The thing that got us about the weekend is that it showed that a hands-on approach to consultation really works."

Justin Wilson
local resident

PRINCIPLES

- People work together in groups around a large map or model. Different groups can deal with different areas or the same area at different scales. Groups can vary in size (10–12 is a good average to aim at).

- Everyone is encouraged to develop their ideas by drawing or making adjustments to a model. Each group needs a facilitator, a note-taker and a mapper (who marks points on a map or plan).

- At the start of the session, participants should choose which group to attend with Team members distributed evenly.

- Each workshop explores the issue allocated to it and prepares a presentation summarising its conclusions.

TIPS

- Using felt-tips and tracing paper is often more suitable than using models because little preparation is needed. On the other hand models can help people visualise in three dimensions, and making a model beforehand can itself generate interest and enthusiasm. The 'Planning for Real' method may be useful (see page **103**).

- Get everyone to sign drawings at the end if controversial or add a key to record consensus points. Draw up a tidy version if necessary.

Design Workshop Props

- [ ] Base maps
- [ ] Tracing paper

or

- [ ] Base model with movable parts
- [ ] Spare cardboard or polystyrene
- [ ] Scissors
- [ ] Post-it notes and cocktail sticks

and

- [ ] Coloured pens (different colours)
- [ ] Attendance sheets
- [ ] Site photographs

Hands-on
Residents and Team members develop design ideas using felt-tip pens and tracing paper laid over a base plan

Design workshop variations

Design workshops, a key creative aspect of most Community Planning Events, can be run in many different ways with a range of different props to suit the subject matter and participants. Here are some possibilities from a number of different events.

Young people
School children join in design workshops using the same materials as adults

Aerial photographs
The view from the air always provides a stimulating perspective

Photos and montages
Views and photomontages help with discussion of design principles

Character cards
Prepared cards showing local design styles help with a workshop on town character

Experts take the lead
Professionals and council officers lead the debate. Often a useful approach for complex technical issues and a guiding principle of Enquiry by Design

Exhibition
Displays of initial proposals and public feedback provide a focus for debate

Flipcharting
Preparing a summary of key conclusions, at the table and to one side; an integral part of design workshops

Plenary report backs

After any working group sessions, there is normally a plenary session where each working group reports back to all the other participants. This ensures that all participants are kept in the picture as the event develops.

PRINCIPLES

- Each working group reports on the findings of its session.

- Each working group decides how best to report its findings and who will make the presentation. It may be one representative of the group or a team effort.

- A record is made of the report back session.

TIPS

- Report backs should be concise and brief and aim to be stimulating and lively.

- Using visuals and prompts on flipcharts will make it more interesting to the audience and make It easier for the presenter. They can also provide a record.

- Presentations are almost invariably more interesting if they are made by local participants rather than by organisers or facilitators. This is also a good way of local people taking ownership of the process outcome.

- It can often work well if groups pin up material on the wall where they are working and the 'audience' move from group space to group space. The alternative is to pin material up on one area of wall or one or more flipcharts and leave the audience where they are.

Summing up
Participants explain workshop conclusions in plenary sessions

"Everybody's voice counts as much as everyone else's. It doesn't matter whether you are the Managing Director of Taylor Woodrow or you just live round the corner. This is about listening and learning from each other."

Steven Pound
Member of Parliament

Taking it in
*Participants listen to reports
from workshop groups*

Team working

Doodling
Sketch on paper tablecloth, made during a Team dinner, which was used in the final report and exhibition

"A bond was created between us. It was like sailing through the bay of Biscay in a great storm. I will be sad to leave. I had a very very good time. Buildings can be more economic if you know who you are building for. I hope very much that I can continue this work in Germany."

Karin-Maria Trautmann
Developer, Berlin

Creative working by members of the Team and others is likely to continue outside of scheduled sessions. Mealtimes and other breaks can be made into a valuable part of the creative process as well as being therapeutic.

PRINCIPLES

- Mealtimes should be stage-managed to ensure maximum opportunities for informal and formal discussion.

- Leisure activities should be built into the event timetable to provide exercise, inspiration and opportunities for some social interaction and networking.

TIPS

- Invite local political, business and community leaders to meals which can end with brief speeches and debate.

- Organise dinners in a variety of inspiring local venues.

- Ensure that paper tablecloths are provided so that people can sketch on the tables during meals.

- A 'brainstorm' during dinner can be very stimulating, especially prior to the main Team editing session. Ask everyone to respond to 2 questions: 'What have you learnt in the past few hours/days?' and 'What are you going to do with it?' Have a flipchart at the ready.

- Saunas, swims, jogs, walks and a late night bar can all be productive.

Working together
Stakeholders collaborate on producing drawings at
an Enquiry by Design event

Brainstorming
Hilltop Team breather, and dinner for Team and
guests, prior to settling down to report production

Report production

The quality of the report of the event will be instrumental in determining what happens next.

Division of labour
Report production roles

PRINCIPLES

- The event report is a collective document of the entire Team. Who contributes what is not important. The aim is to clearly convey the Team's proposals and the rationale behind them.

- The report should be capable of wide distribution and of having a long shelf-life; it may be needed to reignite action in ten years time. Paper and digital (pdf) versions should be produced.

- Ideally, the report should be completed during the event and either printed in time for the final presentation or printed a few days later with a broadsheet produced in the meantime. In practice this may be impractical, especially for shorter events.

- A separate 'event record' or appendices should be produced providing a comprehensive record of the event.

Editing suite
Wall mounted storyboards allow everyone to keep track of progress

TIPS

- A streamlined editing process is essential to produce the report in the time available. Establish clear editorial deadlines and responsibilities. It may be worth having a professional editorial team.

- Adopt a report structure and format at the outset, modifying them later if necessary. Stick to the main issues and be concise. Lengthy reports are unlikely to be read and are too expensive to circulate.

Drawing
Working up design details

- Include all material produced for and at the event in the 'event record'. In the digital age this can easily include Powerpoint presentations, exhibition panels, drawings and workshop notes.

Sample Report Structure

Executive Summary

Introduction
Why the Event was organised
What happens next

Background
Present realities, facts and assumptions

Issues
Main problems and opportunities
analysed

Recommendations
What should be done (short & long term)
Who should do it

Credits
Team members, sponsors,
participants, etc

Sources and notes

Collecting Information Hints

- Three types of information are of most use; statements, quotes and images

- Keep the report structure in mind when collecting information; ie everything should relate to a particular report section

- Keep statements to brief bullet point paragraphs with one or two word headings

- Record general identity of people quoted (eg 'tower block resident') or name and position – in which case check it with them before using

- All copy should have the following information at the top of each page: Originator's initials, typists initials, date, time

Information Flowchart

How information is collected, synthesised and edited for the report

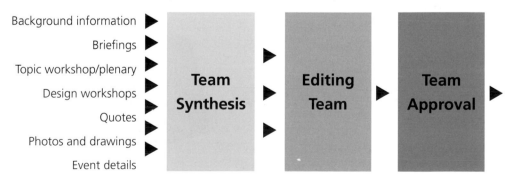

Background information ▶
Briefings ▶
Topic workshop/plenary ▶
Design workshops ▶
Quotes ▶
Photos and drawings ▶
Event details ▶

Team Synthesis ▶ **Editing Team** ▶ **Team Approval** ▶

Sample reports

Published reports are the normal way of refining and disseminating the results of a Community Planning Event, together, perhaps, with a broadsheet for people to take home from the final presentation. Here are some examples of style and content.

Report covers
Plenty of scope for design flair and different formats

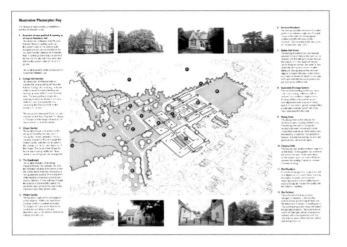

Broadsheet distributed at a final presentation

An A3 folded sheet with the main recommendations, a vision drawing and photos and summary of the process

3 COMMUNITY PLANNING WEEKEND

Inside pages of some event reports and event records

Note the generous use of sketches, plans, diagrams, quotes from participants and photos (of the event as well as of the subject matter)

Public presentation

One of the most exciting and nerve-racking moments of many Community Planning Events is the final presentation.

PRINCIPLES

- The purpose of the presentation is for the Team to present its proposals to the community and then to bow out, leaving the community equipped to take the process forward if it wishes.

- The presentation should be a public event with all those who have been involved particularly encouraged to attend.

- The timing of the presentation is fixed and advertised in advance to provide a deadline which cannot be avoided.

TIPS

- A good format is a Powerpoint presentation, given by the Team Chairperson.

- Create an exhibition round the walls using flipchart sheets, Post-it panels, and other material from the event.

- Make sure there is time for questions and statements from the audience after the presentation.

- Conduct an exit poll to gauge the audience's immediate response.

- A low-key alternative to a formal presentation is an Open House (see page **103**) or simply allow people to view work displayed on the walls.

Monday Evening
8.00pm

REPORT BACK

The Team will be working flat out on Sunday and Monday to turn all the ideas into a Vision for the future

See what you have helped create!

Exhibition • Slide Show

Don't miss it!

Deadline!
Part of an event leaflet

"When I came in this evening I was struck by the sheer amount of creative energy and felt a sense of personal loss that I was not here for all of it."

David Lunts
Councillor

Sample Presentation Structure

1 Brief history of the area covered
2 Description of the Community Planning Event process used
3 Terms of reference for the event
4 Run through of the event process on a day-to-day basis with conclusions drawn out at each stage
5 Vision of what proposals could look like
6 Summary of main recommendations
7 Next steps in the process

Reporting back to the community
Team members present proposals arising from two community planning weekends to packed public sessions at the end of the events

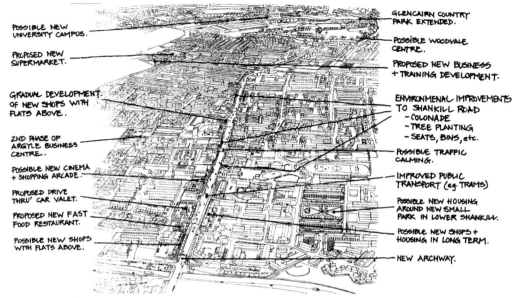

POSSIBLE NEW
UNIVERSITY CAMPUS.

PROPOSED NEW
SUPERMARKET.

GRADUAL DEVELOPMENT
OF NEW SHOPS WITH
FLATS ABOVE.

2ND PHASE OF
ARGYLE BUSINESS
CENTRE.

POSSIBLE NEW CINEMA
+ SHOPPING ARCADE.

PROPOSED DRIVE
THRU' CAR VALET.

PROPOSED NEW FAST
FOOD RESTAURANT.

POSSIBLE NEW SHOPS
WITH FLATS ABOVE.

GLENCAIRN COUNTRY
PARK EXTENDED.

POSSIBLE WOODVALE
CENTRE.

PROPOSED NEW BUSINESS
+ TRAINING DEVELOPMENT.

ENVIRONMENAL IMPROVEMENTS
TO SHANKILL ROAD
  - COLONADE
  - TREE PLANTING
  - SEATS, BINS, etc.

POSSIBLE TRAFFIC
CALMING.

IMPROVED PUBLIC
TRANSPORT (eg. TRAMS)

POSSIBLE NEW HOUSING
AROUND NEW SMALL
PARK IN LOWER SHANKILL.

POSSIBLE NEW SHOPS +
HOUSING IN LONG TERM.

NEW ARCHWAY.

Dream or reality?

Visions arising from two Community Planning Events. Above: regeneration proposals from a community planning weekend in Greater Shankill, Belfast (John Thompson & Partners). Below: a masterplan for a new community of 5,500 new homes, employment, shops and community facilities from an Enquiry by Design in Sherford, Devon (The Prince's Foundation).

Section 5
Follow-up

What next?

Continuing engagement
Walking tour of development under construction

"You shouldn't do one of these things unless you are able to follow up for two to three years at least. Community Planning Events must be the beginning of a process, not isolated events."

Jon Rowland
Chairman
Urban Design Group

The Community Planning Event process does not finish at the end of an event. What happens next is vitally important to ensure that the proposals are acted upon and that the engagement of the community continues during the implementation stage.

PRINCIPLES

- Commitment to follow-up should be built into the process from the beginning and funding allocated.

- The nature of the follow-up will vary depending on local conditions and the extent to which the event is part of an already established development process.

- A definite programme and organisational mechanisms for follow-up should be included in the event report and announced at the presentation. There should be achievable targets and clear responsibilities.

- The local Steering Group, modified as appropriate, should normally take the lead.

TIPS

- Ensure that follow-up is the responsibility of more than one individual, preferably an organisation or local committee.

- Make the follow-up formal and publicise the results.

- Keep good records. Ensure the event report is kept in print, is available on a website and is sent to all relevant organisations and individuals.

- Change the membership of the Steering Group but keep some continuity.

Follow-up Methods

☐ **Implementation workshops**
Organised by the Steering Group on a regular basis to monitor progress

☐ **Report reviews**
Special meetings can be set up to run through the event report with community leaders and others

☐ **Team debriefing**
Perhaps 4-6 weeks after the event. Evaluate event and assess next moves. Preferably in the host community

☐ **Annual evaluation meeting**
Organised by Steering Group or others. Good for maintaining momentum

☐ **Team revisit**
Handful of Team members revisit to:
a) Learn of achievements
b) Offer additional suggestions
c) Prepare an evaluation report
Periodically at intervals. Visits can be formal or informal

☐ **Project website**
Continual updates with opportunities for exchange of views

☐ **Newsletter**
Distributed on a regular basis with updated information on progress

☐ ....

☐ ....

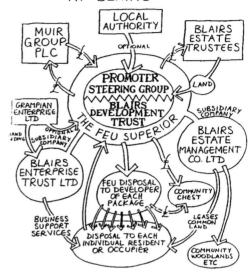

DEVELOPMENT PROCESS FOR URBAN VILLAGE AT BLAIRS

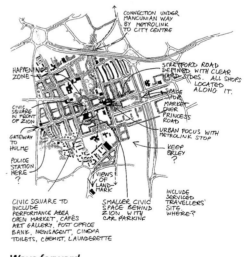

Ways forward
Diagram of proposed development process, and sketch showing urban design proposals, both drawn up at early Community Planning Events and included in the event reports

Evaluation

Real improvements, real communities, real results
New skateboard facility and new eco homes resulting from Community Planning Events

"The ... event was an example of the new collaborations that are emerging ... Our thinking ... has been greatly enriched. Equally importantly, the enthusiasm both of Councillors and officers has been fired anew."

**Nicky Gavron
Chair, Environmental
Services, London
Borough of Haringey**

Evaluating the impact of Community Planning Events helps keep those involved focussed on long-term objectives and is important for improving the process generally.

PRINCIPLES

- Evaluation procedures should be built in from the outset and budgeted for.

- Attempts should be made to evaluate the impact of events even though it will always be difficult to be absolutely certain that any specific changes result directly from an event.

- National or regional evaluations of citizen satisfaction may provide evidence of success but will not replace the need for dedicated evaluation of each event.

- Analysing responses from a range of event participants during and after an event is a practical and valid approach (see form opposite).

TIPS

- People may need incentives to complete evaluation forms. Interviewing will be more reliable but costly.

Common Event Defects

- ☐ Lack of adequate lead time
- ☐ Lack of information at the outset
- ☐ Lack of interest by key players
- ☐ Lack of involvement of all sections of the community
- ☐ Logistical failures of equipment or people
- ☐ Raising expectations without the means to deliver
- ☐ Team members distracted by other commitments
- ☐ Inadequate media coverage
- ☐ Lack of systematic follow-up
- ☐ ....

Community Planning Event Evaluation Form

Complete what you can. Use extra sheets to elaborate but try and summarise in the space provided.

Title of event....

Nature of event...

Place...

Dates of event........................   Date of evaluation...

Name, title and organisation of evaluator...

Role at event (if any)..

Address ....

Telephone ....   Email...

Summarise the impact of the event on the following:

Physical environment (buildings, parks, transport, design standards)............................
....
....

Economy (work prospects, wealth)..
....

Perceptions and aspirations (self-view, hopes)..
....

Local organisations (changed roles, new partnerships)..
....

The participants (members of the public, Team members)...
....

How could the event have been organised better?
....
....

What would be your advice to other communities holding such an event?
....

Any other thoughts
....
....
....

Sample form for evaluating an event. Copy and complete at the end of an event and then again periodically. Ask a range of people who participated in the event to fill it in. Editable version downloadable from the *Toolbox* on **www.communityplanning.net**

Working on the detail together
Design workshop at a Community Planning Event

Appendices

Brief history

Some key moments in the evolution of Community Planning Events.

1967   American Institute of Architects (AIA) responds to citizen in Rapid City, South Dakota, USA and sends a team of architects to look at problems facing the community. Programme of Regional/Urban Design Assistance Teams (R/UDATs) launched by AIA with an average of five events organised each year. Process improved with each experience.

1978   Similar programmes start to be evolved locally in the USA at state level by universities and colleges and by local partnerships including local AIA Chapters. These become generally known as Design Assistance Teams (DATs) although programmes have different names.

1980   AIA starts Generic R/UDAT programme to deal with problems common to many communities. Three events are organised over the next five years.

1981   Planning Assistance Teams programme started by US Air Force using R/UDAT process during weekdays to examine planning issues relating to its bases. 125 events held over next 10 years.

1985   First UK pilot event organised in St Mary's, Southampton by the Royal Institute of British Architects. It is called a Community Urban Design Assistance Team (CUDAT). Attempts to start a similar programme and support service to the AIA fail to get off the ground.

1988   Birmingham's 'Highbury Initiative' introduces 'think tank' style events to the mainstream UK regeneration scene. Handful of UK practitioners and community leaders take part in a joint US/UK team for a Generic R/UDAT in Pittsburgh, USA. It is the largest event ever held and is visited by HRH The Prince of Wales. This leads to a handful of events in the UK organised independently by those who took part.

1989   First UK 'community planning weekend' held at Bishopsgate in London's East End. Duchy of Cornwall hosts 'planning weekend' at Poundbury, Dorchester.

1990   American Institute of Architects produces handbook encouraging others to provide organisational support frameworks at state and local level. Over 100 R/UDATs and several hundred DATs have now been held throughout USA. Urban Design Group organises its first event at Wood Green, London.

1991   UK consultants team up with German group and organise a 'planning week' in Moscow. Urban Design Group organises week-long 'UDAT' in Pereslavl Zalessky near Moscow.

1993   Business in the Community organises its first event at Burgess Park, London. Urban Villages Forum organises its first event at West Silvertown, London.

1994 Urban Design Group announces intention to mount UK support framework.

1995 'Action Planning Task Group' formed by handful of national organisations to coordinate promotion and support services. UK consultants organise events in the Shankill Road, Belfast and at Hellersdorf, East Berlin.

1996 *Action Planning* handbook published by The Prince of Wales's Institute of Architecture. Launch event at St James' Palace, London.

1997 First Middle East event held in Beirut and Sidon.

1999 First Enquiry by Design events organised by The Prince's Foundation at Northampton and Basildon.

2003 First major Stakeholder Participation Day organised for Cambridge Southern Fringe area development framework.

2005 UK Government reinforces need for Community Planning Events in its Planning Policy Statement on Delivering Sustainable Development (PPS1).

2006 First trial Reinvigorate event organised by British Urban Regeneration Association in Bristol.

2008 Publication of *The Community Planning Event Manual*; a revised and updated version of *Action Planning*.

Anything missing? Additional items can be added at **www.communityplanning.net** (site search for Brief history)

Early American experience
Over 125 four-day Community Planning events (R/UDATs) were held throughout the United States under the auspices of the American Institute of Architects between 1967 and 1995. Roughly half dealt with an entire city, a quarter dealt with the central area of a city and the remainder dealt with entire counties, neighbourhoods or open spaces. In addition there were several hundred events organised independently at local level (not marked)

Publications and sources

A selection of material relating to Community Planning Events found useful in compiling this book.

See the *Publications & Film A–Z* and *Websites A–Z* on **www.communityplanning.net** for up-to-date sources of information.

Apart from some of the event reports, items can mostly be obtained from the sources shown in brackets or the organisations listed on page **94**. All material can be consulted at Nick Wates Associates offices by arrangement.

BOOKS & HANDBOOKS

Action Planning for Cities; a guide to community practice, Nabeel Hamdi and Reinhard Goethert, John Wiley & Sons, 1997, 978-0-471-96928-0. Well-illustrated textbook on the theory and practice of community planning in developing countries.

Building Homes People Want; a guide to tenant involvement in the design and development of housing association homes, Pete Duncan and Bill Halsall, National Federation of Housing Associations, 1994. Includes case study of a community planning weekend in Hull, UK.

The Charrette Handbook; the essential guide for accelerated, collaborative community planning, National Charrette Institute, American Planning Association, 2006, 978-1-932364-21-7. Excellent detailed guide for organisers of design charrettes. (From www.charretteinstitute.org)

The Community Planning Handbook; how people can shape their cities, towns & villages in any part of the world, Nick Wates, Earthscan, 2000, 978-1-85383-654-1. Overview of community planning principles and methods. Accessible how-to-do-it style with international scope and relevance.

Creating a Design Assistance Team for Your Community; a guidebook for adapting the American Institute of Architects' Regional/Urban Design Assistance Team (R/UDAT) Program for AIA Components and Chapters, American Institute of Architects, 1990. Useful for support bodies.

Future Search; an action guide to finding common ground in organisations and communities, Marvin Weisboard and Sandra Janoff, Berrett-Kohler, 1995. (From New Economics Foundation)

Making Microplans; a community-based process in design and development, Reinhard Goethert and Nabeel Hamdi, Intermediate Publications, 1988.

Participatory Workshops; a sourcebook of 21 sets of ideas & activities, Robert Chambers, Earthscan, 2002, 978-1-85383-863-7. A wealth of practical tips from a highly experienced practitioner and academic.

Planning your Community's Future; a guide to the Regional/Urban Design Assistance Team Program, American Institute of Architects, 2004. Updated manual for this pioneering programme which has been running since 1967. (Free from www.aia.org)

A Practical Handbook for 'Planning for Real' Consultation Exercises, Neighbourhood Initiatives Foundation, 1995.

Real Time Strategic Change, Robert Jacobs, Berrett-Kohler, 1994.

Sustainable Urban Extensions: Planned through Design; a collaborative approach to developing sustainable town extensions through Enquiry by Design, The Prince's Foundation, 2000, 978-1-898465-26-3. Useful account of early UK experience using Enquiry by Design. (From The Prince's Foundation)

Tools for Partnership-building. How to build development partnerships between the public, private and voluntary sectors. In all central European languages and as a video. Compiled by Ros Tennyson. Prince of Wales Business Leaders Forum, 1994.

Urban Design in Action; the history, theory and development of the American Institute of Architects' Regional/Urban Design Assistance Teams Program (R/UDAT), Peter Batchelor and David Lewis, North Carolina State University School of Design and the American Institute of Architects, 1985. Classic work, currently out of print.

MAGAZINES

Urban Design Quarterly (from Urban Design Group)
No 28, September 1988. Special issue on Community Planning Event issues.
No 41, January 1992. Reports of events in Russia.
No 49, January 1994. Special issue on Community Planning Events titled 'Involving people in urban design'. Articles by: Steve Bee, Jon Billingham, Anthony Costello, David Lewis, Jon Rowland, Alan Simpson, John Thompson, John Worthington and Charles Zucker.
No 58, April 1996. Special issue related to Community Planning Events.
No 67, July 1998. Special issue, 'Involving local communities in urban design'.

THESES & RESEARCH PAPERS

Action Planning, John Worthington, DEGW Group, 1992.

A Community Participation Strategy in Urban Regeneration; case studies in Muirhouse and Greater Pilton, Edinburgh and Hulme – Moss Side, Manchester, Michael Carley, Scottish Homes working paper, 1995. Includes highly informative account and evaluation of a planning weekend.

Designing Livable Communities! the UDAT as an urban design process, Jeremy Caulton, thesis for Joint Centre for Urban Design, Oxford Polytechnic, 1992. Useful study on the transferability of the Community Planning Event technique from USA to UK.

Introduction to the Future Workshop Method, Reinhard Sellnow, shortened translation for ECO 1, Moscow, 1991.

Releasing the Potential of Neighbourhood Regeneration Through Community Participation and Action Planning; the case of Hittin Refugees Settlement in Russefa – Jordon. Firas Sharaf, Dissertation at the University of York, 1996.

What is a Community Planning Weekend? John Thompson, John Thompson & Partners, 1995.

EVENT REPORTS

A Case for Collaboration, Miles Platting & Ancoats Action Planning Team, 26–28 January 1995.

Cities Don't Just Happen, Wood Green UDAT; London Borough of Haringey, 1990.

Blairs College Community Planning Weekend; a sustainable settlement for Grampian, Muir Group, 1994.

Boise R/UDAT, Central Idaho chapter AIA, 1985.

Cambridge East Area Action Plan Stakeholder Consultation Day Event Record, Cambridge City Council and South Cambridgeshire District Council, 2005.

Central Avenue Study, Albuquerque, New Mexico, R/UDAT report, 1984.

Cherry Knowle Hospital; Enquiry by Design, The Prince's Foundation, 2003.

Creating the new heart of Hulme, Hulme Regeneration Ltd., 1992.

ECO-1 International Community Planning Week, European Academy of the Urban Environment, Berlin, 1992.

Greater Shankill Community Planning Weekend, Greater Shankill Partnership, February 1995.

Internationaler Planning Workshop, Berlin – Hellersdorf, WoGeHe, 1995.

The Highbury Initiative; Birmingham City Centre Challenge Symposium, 25–27 March 1988, DEGW/URBED.

Imagine, Anderson, Indiana, R/UDAT report, AIA, 1985

Last Place in the Downtown Plan, AIA R/UDAT team, report of R/UDAT in Portland, Oregon, 1983.

Mitten in Lubeck, Ergebnisse der Perspektivenwerkstatt, von Zadow, 2007

The Newcastle Initiative; Theatre Village Study, RIBA Northern Branch, October 1988.

Poundbury Planning Weekend, Duchy of Cornwall, (report and appendices), 1989.

Remaking the Monongahela Valley, R/UDAT report, AIA, 1988.

Report of the Burgess Park Urban Design Action Team, 29–30 Jan 1993, Business in the Community.

Runnymede Campus Community Planning Weekend, 2007, John Thompson & Partners

St Mary Street, Southampton; CUDAT report, Royal Institute of British Architects, 1985.

Sherford New Community Enquiry by Design, 4–6 October 2004, Summary report, The Prince's Foundation.

Traffic Management in Hastings Old Town; an agenda for action, Dr Carmen Hass-Klau, Dr Graham Crampton and Nick Wates (eds), Hastings Urban Conservation Project and Hastings Old Town Forum, 1989.

West Silvertown Planning Weekend, Urban Villages Forum, 1993.

Contacts

Some contacts for further information and support on Community Planning Events.

See the *Contacts A–Z* and *Websites A–Z* on **www.communityplanning.net** for up-to-date sources of information.

The Academy of Urbanism
70 Cowcross Street, London, EC1M 6EJ, UK
t + f +44 (0)20 7251 8777
e lg@academyofurbanism.org.uk
w www.academyofurbanism.org.uk
High-level, cross-sector group of individuals from a wide range of disciplines, brought together to champion the cause of good quality urbanism throughout Great Britain and Ireland.

American Institute of Architects (AIA)
1735 New York Avenue, NW
Washington DC 20006, USA
t +1 202 626 7300 **f** 626 7547
e infocentral@aia.org or rudat@aia.org
w www.aia.org
The Institute's Centre for Communities by Design promotes design assistance team (DAT) programmes. Has films, tapes, brochures and reports from US events. Supplies addresses of experienced team members and local and state support programmes.

Association DIALOG
6, rue de Touraine, 67 100 Strasbourg, France
e dialog.assoc@gmail.com
w www.dialog-France.org
Contact: Eléonore Hauptmann, Urban planner, Chairman
Non-profit organisation developing new practices in citizen involvement to improve the relationships between human beings and the environment. Producer of French version of this book.

British Urban Regeneration Association (BURA)
63-66 Hatton Garden, London, EC1N 8LE, UK
t 0800-0181-260 **f** 020-7404-9614
e info@bura.org.uk
w www.bura.org.uk
Forum for the exchange of ideas, experience and information for the regeneration sector. Promotes collaborative processes including Reinvigorate.

Centre for Development & Emergency Practice (CENDEP)
Oxford Brookes University, Gypsy Lane Campus, Headington, Oxford, OX3 0BP, UK
t 01865 483413 **f** 483298
e cendep@brookes.ac.uk
w www.brookes.ac.uk/schools/be/cendep/
Contact: Nabeel Hamdi
Postgraduate programme. Expertise on community planning, particularly in developing countries.

Development Trusts Association
33 Corsham Street, London, N1 6DR, UK
t +44 (0)845 458 8336 **f** 458 8337
e info@dta.org.uk
w www.dta.org.uk
National UK umbrella organisation for community-based development organisations. Useful publications, training and information exchange.

Earthscan
Dunstan House, 14a St Cross Street, London, EC1N 8XA, UK
t +44 (0) 20 7841 1930 **f** 7242 1474
e publisher@earthscan.co.uk
w www.earthscan.co.uk
UK-based publisher of books on sustainable development including a 'Tools for community planning' suite.

English Partnerships
110 Buckingham Palace Road, London, SW1W 9SA, UK
t + 44 (0)20 7881 1600 **f** 7730 9162
e mail@englishpartnerships.co.uk
w www.englishpartnerships.co.uk
National regeneration agency helping to support high-quality sustainable growth in England.

John Thompson & Partners
Wren House, 43 Hatton Garden, London, EC1N 8EL, UK
t +44 (0)20 7405 1211 **f** 7405 1221
e jtplon@jtp.co.uk
w www.jtp.co.uk
Architects, urban designers and community planners with much experience of participatory community planning methods in the UK and Europe. Community Planning Weekends a speciality.

National Charrette Institute (NCI) (USA)
3439 NE Sandy Blvd. #349, Portland, OR 97232
t +1 (503) 233-8486 **f** 233-1811
e info@charretteinstitute.org
w www.charretteinstitute.org
Non-profit educational institution which teaches 'the transformative process of Dynamic Planning to create healthy community plans'. Website contains explanations, toolkits and other resources for planning and running charrettes.

Neighbourhood Initiatives Foundation
The Poplars, Lightmoor, Telford, TF4 3QN, UK
t +44 (0)1952 590777 **f** 591771
e info@nif.co.uk **w** www.nif.co.uk
Charity specialising in community participation, training and development, often using 'Planning for Real' which is a registered trademark of the Foundation. Has membership scheme, regular newsletter, training courses and useful publications and packs.

New Economics Foundation
3 Jonathan Street, London, SE11 5NH, UK
t +44 (0)20 7820 6300 **f** 7820 6301
e info@neweconomics.org
w www.neweconomics.org
Promotes community visioning, indicators, community finance and social audits. Coordinates UK Participation Network.

Nick Wates Associates
Creative Media Centre, 45 Robertson Street, Hastings, TN34 1HL, UK
t +44 (0)1424 205446 **f** 205401
e info@nickwates.co.uk
w www.nickwates.co.uk
Editors of this handbook. Provides consultancy on process management.

Post-war Reconstruction and Development Unit
University of York, Heslington, York, YO10 5DD, UK
t +44 (0)1904 432640 **f** 432641
w www.york.ac.uk/depts/poli/prdu
Contact: Sultan Barakat
Community planning expertise in post-war situations.

The Prince's Foundation
19–22 Charlotte Road, Shoreditch, London, EC2A 3SG, UK
t +44 (0)20 7916 7380 **f** 7916 7381
e projects@princes-foundation.org
w www.princes-foundation.org
Unites and extends HRH The Prince of Wales's initiatives in architecture, building and urban regeneration. Encourages a holistic and humane approach to the planning and design of communities. Pioneered the Enquiry by Design (EbD) process and can provide advice and assistance for those wishing to use it. Website has downloadable information on EbD including case studies (Projects & Practice section).

Urban Design Group
70 Cowcross Street, London, EC1M 6EJ, UK
t 020 7250 0872
e admin@udg.org.uk **w** www.udg.org.uk
National UK voluntary organisation that helps set urban design agenda.

URBED
26 Gray's Inn Road, London, WC1X 8HP, UK
t +44 (0)20 7831 9986 **f** 7831 2466
e urbed@urbed.com **w** www.urbed.com
Urban regeneration consultants with long experience of community planning. Expertise in round table workshops.

Vista Consulting
16 Old Birmingham Road, Lickey End, Bromsgrove, B60 1DE, UK
t +44 (0)1527 837930 f 837940
e enquiries@vista.uk.com **w** www.vista.uk.com
Information and consultancy on critical mass events such as real-time strategic change.

VON ZADOW GmbH - JTP Europe
Geschwister-Scholl-Str. 31 b, D-14548 Schwielowsee, Germany
t + 49 (33209) 20833 **f** +49 (33209) 20834
e info@vonzadow.de **w** www.vonzadow.de
Contact: Andreas von Zadow
Development companions for sustainable development in cities, communities and organisations. Producer of German and French versions of this book.

Early events listing

Some pioneering Community Planning Events held in the UK (or elsewhere with strong UK involvement) between 1985 and 1995. Details of some more recent events can be found in the *Projects A–Z* on www.communityplanning.net

Date	Name/Place	Nature
5/85	St Mary's Southampton	Inner city regeneration
3/88	Highbury Initiative, Birmingham	New vision for entire city
3/88	Mon Valley, Pittsburgh, USA	Redundant steel industry valley regeneration
10/88	Theatre Village, Newcastle	Central city regeneration
11/88	Maiden Lane, London	Modern housing estate improvements
1/89	Bishopsgate, London	Redundant railway land redevelopment
6/89	Poundbury, Dorchester	New settlement proposal
10/89	Wornington Green, London	Housing estate improvements
11/89	Old Town, Hastings	Traffic improvements in historic town
4/90	Wood Green, London	New vision for metropolitan district
7/90	Cape Hill, Sandwell	'Radburn' housing estate redesign
9/90	Kings Cross, London	Alternative plan for key inner city site
11/90	Smethwick, Sandwell	Inner City Renewal Area
7/91	North Hull, Kingston-Upon-Hull	Housing estates improvements
4/91	East Finchley, London	Redundant factory site reuse
5/91	Pereslavl, Russia	Provincial historic town planning proposals
5/91	ECO 1, Moscow	Metropolitan district planning proposals
8/91	Penwith Manor Estate, Lambeth	Housing estates improvements
5/92	St Helier, Jersey	Neighbourhood regeneration
11/92	Hulme, Manchester	Inner city regeneration
1/93	Burgess Park, Southwark, London	District park regeneration
2/93	Castle Vale, Birmingham	Vision for housing area on city outskirts
8/93	Angell Town, Brixton, London	Housing estate improvements
12/93	West Silvertown, London	Urban village proposal for docklands
4/94	Barcelona, Spain	Principles of sustainable development
5/94	Hammersmith Broadway, London	Inner city neighbourhood regeneration
6/94	Blairs College, Aberdeen	New sustainable settlement proposal
6/94	Muirhouse, Edinburgh	Housing estate regeneration
9/94	Rocester, Staffordshire	Housing site in village centre proposals
12/94	Turin, Italy	Ecological inner city regeneration
1/95	Miles Platting, Manchester	Inner city industrial area regeneration
2/95	Shankill Road, Belfast	Inner city regeneration
9/95	Blairs College, Aberdeen	Vision for university village proposal
10/95	Hellersdorf, East Berlin	Vision for system-built mass housing estate
11/95	Rochdale, Yorkshire	Mixed use canalside regeneration scheme

Eligibility Events listed have followed fairly closely the process outlined in this book, or have been described as Community Planning Events, planning weekends or urban design assistance teams. Many excellent but more general community planning exercises, including 'Planning for Real' events have not been included.

* Events held over more than one weekend.

Length	Host/Organiser/Chairperson or Coordinator
3 days	St Mary Street Group & City of Southampton/RIBA/Richard Burton
3 days*	Birmingham City & DoE's City Action Team/URBED & DEGW/Nicholas Falk
5 days	American Institute of Architects/John P Clarke
5 days	RIBA (Northern)/Newcastle Initiative/Neil Barker, Alan Simpson & JT
5 days	London Borough of Camden/HTA/JT
5 days	London & Edinburgh Trust/ Environment Trust & HTA /JT & Jon Aldenton
5 days	Duchy of Cornwall/HTA/JT
5 days	Kensington Housing Trust/HTA/JT
1 day	Hastings Old Town Forum/Urban Conservation Project/Nick Wates
2 days	Haringey Council/Urban Design Group/John Worthington
5 days	Sandwell Metropolitan Borough Council/HTA/JT
5 days	Kings Cross Team/HTA/JT
5 days	Sandwell Metropolitan Borough Council/HTA/JT
2 days*	North Hull Housing Action Trust
5 days	local Labour Party & youth group/Will Hudson
5 days	Cultural Institute for Independent Analysis/UDG/Arnold Linden
11 days	European Academy of the Urban Environment/Slava Glazychev/AvZ & JT
5 days	London Borough of Lambeth/HTA/JT
5 days	States of Jersey/Mason Design Partnership and HTA/Derek Mason & JT
5 days	Hulme Regeneration Ltd/HTA/JT
2 days	Business in the Community/DEGW/John Worthington
4 days*	Castle Vale Housing Action Trust/HTA/JT
5 days	London Borough of Lambeth/HTA/JT
5 days	London Docklands Development Corporation/Urban Villages Forum/JT
7 days	City of Barcelona/EAUE/Andreas von Zadow & JT
2 days	Hammersmith Community Trust/Vision for London/David Lewis
5 days	John Muir Group/HTA/JT
5 days	The Northwest Edinburgh Area Renewal/Vance Allen Associates
2 days	The Planning Cooperative/Ian Davison
7 days	City of Turin/Softech/EAUE/Antonella Marruco & AvZ & JT
3 days	Miles Platting Development Trust/Business in the Community/JW
5 days	Greater Shankill Partnership/John Thompson & Partners/JT
4 days	John Muir Group/JTP/JT
5 days	Wohnungsbaugesellschaft (WoGeHe) Hellersdorf/JTP/JT
5 days	Rochdale Partnership/JTP/JT

Abbreviations

AvZ	Andreas von Zadow	JT	John Thompson
EAUE	European Academy of the Urban Environment	JTP	John Thompson & Partners
		JW	John Worthington
HTA	Hunt Thompson Associates	UDG	Urban Design Group

Case study snapshots

Summaries of some Community Planning Events indicating the impact of different approaches
In date order. For detailed examples, see the *Case Studies* section and *Projects A–Z* on
www.communityplanning.net

TITLE, LOCATION, DATE AND NATURE OF EVENT	OUTCOME
North Downtown area, Portland, Oregon, USA, 1983 Standard 4-day R/UDAT organised by the American Institute of Architects to explore future possibilities for a neglected part of the central business district.	A new local business association was formed immediately and a follow-up policy report, based on the event's proposals for land use and transport, was adopted by the City authorities two years later. A local property owners' association was formed in 1986 which produced an improvement programme for historic areas. In 1988, a Downtown development programme released by the City stated that the event had 'stimulated considerable interest in the North Downtown Area which led to the establishment of several area organisations, and inspired further in-depth studies by the Planning Bureau.'
	An evaluation in 1992 – nine years after the R/UDAT event – states that the event's report was 'still being used by city hall'. 'Individual developers now use the UDAT study regularly to interest investors in the area's potential ... whilst the recommendations on transportation and infrastructure improvements are being actively pursued through collaborations between the city authority and community and business interests'. [1]
The Highbury Initiative, Birmingham, UK, 1988 3-day event to provide a new vision for the entire city. Hosted by the City Council and funded by the Department of the Environment's City Action Team.	The proposals produced by the event were adopted by the City Council as a provisional strategy for the city centre. The event also led to the City Engineer downgrading the inner city ring road and giving pedestrians priority.
	A subsequent event one year later led to the formation of a special council committee to deal with the city centre, the setting up of associations for different neighbourhoods and the appointment of consultants to prepare urban design guidelines for them.
	An evaluation in 1995 concludes: 'The event succeeded in generating a new vision, shifting the agenda and priorities and enlisting new energy. The work of the City Council in transforming the centre, with for example extensive public art, has helped to stem decline and boost investment prospects, and has been widely acclaimed by those who have seen the results.' [2]

1. *R/UDAT Handbook* and Alan Simpson and Charles Zucker in *Urban Design Quarterly* No 49, January 1994.
2. Nicholas Falk, URBED, letter to the editor, 24 January 1995.

Traffic Management Study Day, Hastings Old Town, 1989
1-day event to resolve traffic problems. Organised for a partnership of local groups by a local urban regeneration project.

The event resulted in proposals for a range of traffic calming measures which had not previously been thought of and which were unanimously agreed by all parties. Shortly afterwards the Borough's traffic officer was sent on a traffic calming training course. Local residents established a special working party and campaigned successfully for, and helped design, traffic calming measures in one street. Another strategic traffic calming measure was undertaken by the Borough and the County Council.

Castle Vale Community Planning Weekend, Birmingham, 1993
5-day event as part of an 8-week consultation exercise on the future of a 1960s estate of 5,000 homes on the city outskirts. Commissioned by the Department of the Environment prior to tenants voting whether to form a Housing Action Trust.

The event helped residents establish a strategic vision for improvements to the estate and was followed by the highest ever recorded vote in favour of forming a housing action trust to take over management from the local authority.

A second, 2-day, community planning weekend was held to develop a physical masterplan; testing out proposals from the first event and those developed by the architects to ensure that the masterplan was fully in tune with what both local residents and local officials wanted. The masterplan has since been adopted in its entirety by the Housing Action Trust.

West Silvertown Community Planning Weekend, London Docklands, 1993
5-day event organised by the Urban Villages Forum to test the idea of establishing an urban village on redundant dockland.

The event Team supported the proposal and the event helped to galvanise interest. Specific design ideas were generated, some of which later found their way into the developers' brief for the site. Funds were raised to help establish a local development trust. The event was also a useful action learning process for the Urban Villages Forum which went on to use the experience in projects elsewhere.

Greater Shankill Planning Weekend, Belfast, 1995
5-day event to plan a vision for the future of an inner city area particularly affected by the conflict in Northern Ireland.

The event attracted 600 people including representatives from 62 community groups, 45 public, statutory and private agencies and 5 political parties. It galvanised the Greater Shankill Partnership, representing a wide range of local interests, to prepare a funding bid for a £27 million regeneration project which, at the time of going to press, has been shortlisted by the Millennium Commission.

Case study snapshots contd.

Caterham Barracks Community Planning Weekend, Surrey, 1998
4-day event followed by continuous community engagement throughout the planning stages. See **www.communityplanning.net** Case Study for more details.

An impressive example of a private developer using consensus-led masterplanning to create a new sustainable community. Over 1,000 local people were involved in an initial vision-building community planning weekend held on the site, a former army barracks with several historic (Grade II listed) buildings. The completed scheme is an economically integrated, mixed use neighbourhood that includes housing (366 homes for sale and for rent), supermarket, offices, veterinary hospital, surgery, indoor skateboard and BMX centre, and open space. A new community development trust manages leisure and business facilities and creates jobs for local people.

Upton Urban Extension Enquiry by Design, Northampton, 1999
Masterplan for a sustainable urban extension with over 1,000 new homes. See **www.communityplanning.net** Case Study for more details. More Enquiry by Design cases on **www.princes-foundation.org**

A highly successful new urban development. In its structure Upton breaks from previous planning presumptions towards zoned, mono-use similar to previous developments in the area (dominated by housing estates and business parks) and instead has a permeable network of streets and public space, engendering community and offering – in its range of residential, retail, education and employment uses – a real opportunity to mitigate car dependency for residents. It has been recognised as an exemplar of sustainable building in three separate award schemes.

Aylesham Masterplan Enquiry by Design, Kent, 2003
Enquiry by Design process used to develop a masterplan to expand a declining village. See **www.communityplanning.net** Case Study for more details.

The Enquiry by Design process helped the multidisciplinary professional team to produce a draft masterplan which received widespread public and stakeholder support during a subsequent consultation phase. The vast majority of Aylesham residents (83%) supported the plans for village development overall. The Masterplan was formally adopted by the authorities relatively quickly and was used to guide development by private developers.

Cambridge Southern Fringe Stakeholder Participation Day, 2003
1-day event to allow interested parties input into plans for the area's future. Part of drawing up a Draft Area Development Framework for the Local Plan. See **www.scambs.gov.uk** and **www.cambridge.gov.uk** for latest info. Event report from **www.nickwates.co.uk** (Reports & Brochures).

The day caused a huge amount of information to be assembled on plans by various landowners and authorities which had not previously been available. All this and the results of the event were made available in an event report which was circulated to all participants and made available on the internet. Significant alterations resulted in proposals by developers as a result of workshops at the event. The authorities were so pleased with the result that they organised an almost identical event two years later for the Eastern side of the city. The results of both events fed into the Local Plan (Local Development Framework).

Sherford New Community Enquiry by Design, 2004
Masterplanning for a sustainable new urban community with over 5,500 new homes. See **www.redtreellp.com** or **www.princes-foundation.org** for more information.

Masterplan with planning permission for a new community containing up to 5,500 new homes, up to 7,000 new jobs and a 207 hectare Community Park. One of the largest habitat creation schemes in the South West of England. The layout is moulded to the varying topography of the site, retaining as many of the key landscape features as possible, and structured as a series of walkable neighbourhoods – where most residents are within a 5-minute walk from their daily shopping needs. Higher intensity retail and employment will be located in a new high street. The Masterplan aims to set new standards for sustainability in terms of resource efficiency, increased use of renewables, public transport provision and sustainable urban form and it is accompanied by a Town Code which seeks to ensure quality delivery of urbanism and architecture grounded in local tradition and ecological principles.

Heart of East Greenwich collaborative design workshop 2005
1-day event to explore design proposals for a strategic city site, preceded by an open house event and followed by a public report back session. See **www.communityplanning.net** Case Study for more information.

Comprehensive and creative consultation approach to preparing a development brief and selecting a developer for an urban site of strategic local importance. Illustrates how early and ongoing engagement can draw positively on community knowledge to inform and influence the design and how community engagement can be a central and integral part of the whole design and procurement process.

Bristol Reinvigorate, 2007
1-day event to explore the best ways of regenerating two inner city neighbourhoods. See **www.communityplanning.net** Case Study for more details.

Pilot of the interesting Reinvigorate technique of bringing 'outside' and 'inside' expertise together for a day to generate ideas and momentum. The problems and opportunities of two neighbourhoods in the city were mapped out and broad consensus reached on a number of initiatives needed. Mostly these reinforced the approach already being adopted by local stakeholders. Both insiders and outsiders found the event a useful and stimulating experience.

Lübeck Community Planning Weekend, Germany, 2007
5-day event to to find the best and most widely accepted solution for redesigning and enlarging the central pedestrian area of a historic European town and World Heritage Site. See **www.communityplanning.net** Case Study for more details.

Productive use of a Community Planning Weekend to find the best and most widely accepted solution for redesigning and enlarging the central pedestrian area of a historic European town and World Heritage Site. The results were received enthusiastically by the public at the final presentation and the final event report forms part of the brief for an international design competition for the redesign of the pedestrian zone.

Glossary

An explanation of the sometimes confusing terminology used in the field of Community Planning Events. See *Glossary A–Z* on www.communityplanning.net for a more comprehensive list of terms used in community planning, regeneration and environmental sustainability.

Action Planning
Similar meaning to *Community Planning Event.* Term used as title for first edition of this book.

Capacity Building Workshop
Event organised primarily to establish partnerships between the public, private and voluntary sectors on development issues.

Charrette
See **Design Charrette.**

Collaborative Design Workshop
Similar to *design workshop* or *design charrette.* Term used in this book for a 1-day workshop sandwiched between an *open house event* and public report back session (see page **52**).

Community Planning
Planning carried out with the active participation of the end users. Similarly *community architecture, community design* and so on.

Community Planning Event
Carefully structured collaborative event at which all stakeholders, including the local community, work closely with specialists from all relevant disciplines to make plans for the future of that community or some aspects of it.

Community Planning Weekend
Term most commonly used in the UK for a Community Planning Event spanning a weekend. First used in 1989 at Bishopsgate, London. The term **Planning Weekend** is also used. Terms **Planning Week** and **Community Planning Week** have also been used for slightly longer events. Also **Community Planning Day.**

Community Visioning
Term used to describe methods for getting communities to think and plan ahead.

Consultation Day
See **Stakeholder Participation Day.**

Critical Mass Event
Umbrella term for organisation development techniques involving large-scale events often lasting several days and often involving hundreds of people. Mostly used for organisational change but may also be appropriate for community planning. Labels given to specific types of event – structured in different ways and promoted by different people – include **Future Search Conference, Large-Scale Interactive Process, Conference Model, Real-Time Strategic Change, Participative Work Redesign** and **Open-Space Meetings**.

Design Assistance Team (DAT)
Term used by the American Institute of Architects to describe state-level Community Planning Events. These evolved from the Institute's 20-year national level **Regional/Urban Design Assistance Team (R/UDAT)** programme (see below). Similar terms in use include **Urban Design Assistance Team (UDAT)** and **Housing Assistance Team (HAT)** (where only housing involved). Local **DAT** programmes have a wide variety of names; for example Ontario's **Community Assist/Urban Study Effort (CAUSE)** and Mississippi's **Small Town Action Team (STAT)**. First UK event was called a **Community/Urban Design Assistance Team (CUDAT)**.

Design Charrette
Intensive design session, often including 'all-nighter', originally just for architecture students but more recently including the public and professionals. Term originated at the Paris Ecole des Beaux-Arts at the turn of the century. Projects were collected at designated times on a cart ('charrette') where students would be found putting finishing touches to their schemes. Term now widely used in the USA to describe any intensive, group brainstorming effort. **Charrette** now often used without the 'Design' in front.

Design Day
Day when architects and local people brainstorm for design solutions to particular building

problems, usually in teams. Term also used to describe day when local residents can drop in and talk through design ideas with professionals.

Design Workshop
Hands-on session allowing groups to work creatively developing planning and design options. Sometimes called **Hands-on Planning.**

Enquiry by Design
Intensive workshop process involving urban designers and local stakeholders. Devised for developing plans for new build and regeneration by The Prince's Foundation (see page **95**).

Focus Group
Small group of people who work through an issue in workshop sessions. Membership may be carefully selected or entirely random.

Future Workshop
Term used for a workshop devised to discuss options for the future. Various formats possible.

Open House
Event designed to allow those promoting development initiatives to present them to a wider public and secure reactions in an informal manner. Halfway between an exhibition and a workshop.

Planning for Real
Technique for community involvement in planning and development focussing on the construction and use of flexible cardboard models and priority cards. Promoted and branded by the Neighbourhood Initiatives Foundation (page **95**).

Planning Assistance Team (PAT)
Similar to *Design Assistance Team*. Event programme started by US Air Force using R/UDAT process on weekdays for planning issues relating to its bases.

Planning Weekend
See **Community Planning Weekend**.

Reinvigorate
Event usually lasting one day where 'outsiders' and 'insiders' undertake a workshop process to identify solutions to an area's problems. Process developed by the British Urban Regeneration Agency (BURA) (see page **94**).

Regional/Urban Design Assistance Team (R/UDAT)
Name originally given to the Community Planning Event programme started by the American Institute of Architects in 1967. A **generic R/UDAT** uses the same process to look at problems common to many communities. A **mini R/UDAT** uses a similar process with a student team.

Stakeholder
Person or organisation with an interest because they will be affected or may have some influence.

Stakeholder Participation Day
One-day Community Planning Event. Sometimes called a *Consultation Day*.

Study Day
Day spent examining a particular issue. Useful for simple issues.

Task Force
Multidisciplinary team of students and professionals who produce in-depth proposals for a site or neighbourhood based on an intensive programme of site studies, lectures, participatory exercises and studio working, normally lasting several weeks. See *Methods A–Z* on **www.communityplanning.net**

Think Tank
Brainstorming group. Mainly used by governments and city authorities. Often for 'experts' only. May use a Community Planning Event format. Sometimes called an **Expert Panel** or **Symposium.**

Urban Design Action Team
Term adopted by the Urban Design Group for its first UK Community Planning Event in 1990 and used again since. (Note the American 'Assistance' has changed to 'Action' – see **Design Assistance Team**.)

Workshop
Meeting at which a small group, perhaps aided by a facilitator, explores issues, develops ideas and makes decisions. A less formal and more creative counterpart to public meetings and committees. A **Topic Workshop** focusses on specific issues. A **Design Workshop** includes the use of participatory design techniques.

Flowchart perspectives

Visualisations by experienced consultants of Community Planning Events and how they fit within the overall development process. The context for each event will be different with the event format designed accordingly.

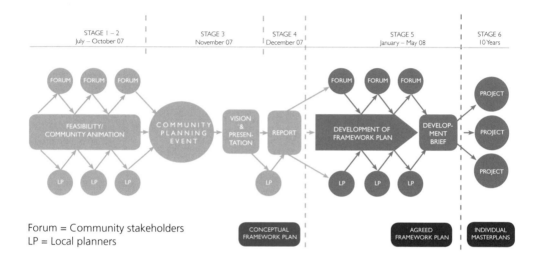

Forum = Community stakeholders
LP = Local planners

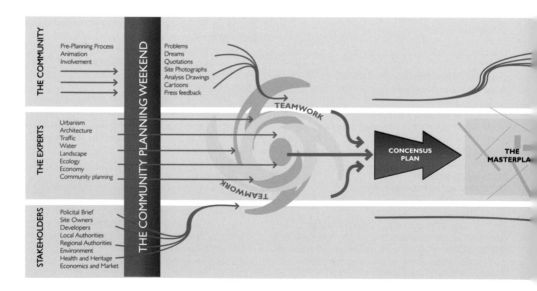

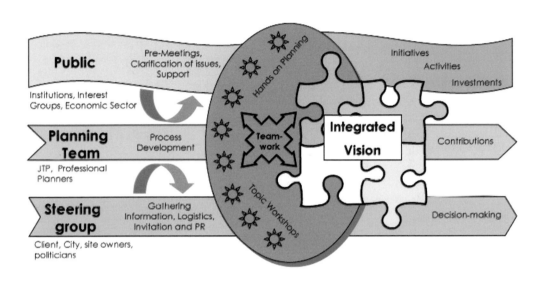

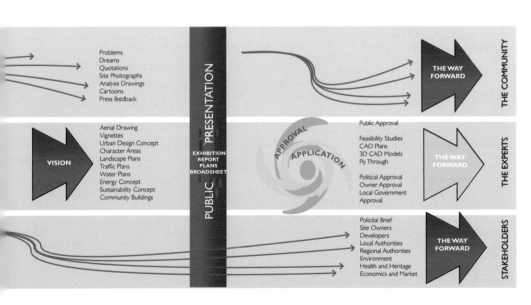

Community Planning Event summary

An aid to thinking about your own event. See also the planner on the next spread.

SAMPLE (based on example page **15**)

Location	Anytown
Reason for Community Planning Event	Decline of traditional industry. Lack of investment in housing. Unemployment. Derelict sites. Uncertainty. Despondency
Aims of initiative	New sense of vision. Programmes of action, long and short term. Sustainability
Type of event	Planning weekend
Length of event	4 days
Lead time	5 months
Timing of event	Second weekend in April next year
Related initiatives	Sustainability conference. Developers' deadline for town centre
Organiser	Anytown Environment Network
Associate organisers	National Urban Trust
Supporters	Anytown Council & Chamber of Commerce
Approximate cost	£20,000 to £50,000
Funding sources	Shell, Greenpeace, local firms
Administration	Architects Company
Support bodies	National Urban Trust
Technical support team	Anytown College Urban Design Department
Team Chairperson	Sally Facilitator
Team members	John Engineer, Jane Ecologist, Simon Urbanist, Jenny Economist, Mark Editor
Follow-up responsibility	Anytown Environment Network
Other	Possibility of link-up with the government's urban design campaign

YOUR EVENT

Location ....

Reason for Community Planning Event ....
....
....

Aims of initiative ....
....

Type of event ....

Length of event ....

Lead time ....

Timing of event ....

Related initiatives ....
....

Organiser ....
....

Supporters ....

Approximate cost ....

Funding sources ....

Administration ....
....

Technical support team ....

Team Chairperson ....

Team members ....
....

Follow-up responsibility ....

Other ....
....

Community Planning Event planner

To help start shaping any kind of Community Planning Event (or thinking through whether one would be useful at all). Can be used in a workshop session after a presentation, or as part of a training exercise.

AIMS

1. What do you want to **achieve** from a Community Planning Event?

....

2. What are the **main issues** to be addressed?

....

3. What geographical **area** should it cover?

....

NATURE OF EVENT

4. How **long** should the event (or events) be?

....

5. **When** should the event be? (dates)

....

6. What **specific activities** should take place, and in what order?

....

7. Who are the **key people** to invite?

....

8. Should there be an **independent team** of facilitators from outside the area? YES/NO
9. If YES what **expertise** do you want on the team?

....

10. Any ideas for names of **Team members** or the **Team Chairperson**?

....

ORGANISATION

11. Which organisation/s should **host** the event?

....

12. Who else should **help** and how?

....

13. Who will do the **administration**?

....

14. **Where** should the event be held?
    Workshops? ....
    Presentations? ....
    Meals? ....
    Hotels? ....

15. What **briefing material** should be made available or prepared?

....

16. Who will make sure that the results of the event are used and built on **afterwards**?

....

MONEY

17. How much will it **cost** (roughly)?

Admin	£/$......
Venues	£/$......
Publicity	£/$......
Catering	£/$......
Equipment	£/$......
Photography	£/$......
Travel	£/$......
Accommodation	£/$......
Report printing	£/$......
Website building	£/$......
Fees and wages	£/$......
Follow-up activity	£/$......
Other	£/$......
Total	£/$......

18. Who might **sponsor** it (or do things free)?

....
....
....
....
....
....
....
....
....
....
....
....
....

IMMEDIATE NEXT STEPS

19. **Who** does **what** now?

....
....
....

OTHER THOUGHTS AND IDEAS

20. ....
....
....
....
....

Name and contact details (optional)

....
....

Date......................

Download a template of this form in Rich Text format from the *Toolbox* on
www.communityplanning.net

Acknowledgements

This handbook was first produced as part of the Tools for Community Design programme which was supported by The Prince of Wales's Institute of Architecture (POWIA). The programme was developed by Nick Wates in association with Ros Tennyson and John Thompson under the guidance of the Institute's Director of Research, Professor Keith Critchlow and Director, Dr Richard John.

The editor would like to acknowledge in particular the work of the American Institute of Architects whose programme of Regional & Urban Design Assistance Teams (R/UDATs) pioneered the Community Planning Event approach. Special thanks are also due to Jeremy Caulton for his invaluable thesis on the transferability of the technique, English Partnerships and Inner City Aid for providing financial support and all those who provided material, participated in the 1995 and 2007 'Editing Days' or commented on drafts. They include:

Mel Agace, *Practical Projects Co-ordinator, POWIA*
Jon Allen, *Research Co-ordinator, POWIA*
Harriet Baldwin, *English Partnerships*
Sultan Barakat, *Director, Post-war Reconstruction and Development Unit, Institute of Architectural Studies, York*
Michael Baynes, *Development Surveyor, Hawk Development Management plc*
Dianah Bennett, *librarian*
John Billingham, *Editor, Urban Design Quarterly*
Jeff Bishop, *Director, BDOR Ltd*
Ben Bolgar, *Director of Design, Theory & Networks, The Prince's Foundation*
Georgina Burke, *Senior Corporate Marketing Executive, English Partnerships*
Charles Campion, *John Thompson & Partners*
Jeremy Caulton, *Senior Consultant, Urban Initiatives*
Caroline Clark, *Regeneration Unit, Civic Trust*
Jessica Courtney Bennett, *Programmes Assistant, British Urban Regeneration Association*
Rob Cowan, *writer and consultant on urban affairs*
Keith Critchlow, *Director of Research, POWIA*
Alastair Dick-Cleland, *student, POWIA*
Peter Eley, *Architect*
Nicholas Falk, *Director, URBED urban & economic development group*
Richard Feilden, *Chairman, Community Architecture Group, Royal Institute of British Architects*

Nicola Forde, *John Thompson & Partners*
Stephen Gallagher, *British Urban Regeneration Association*
Alan and Joanna Gent, *teachers*
Tony Gibson, *consultant*
Keith Gillies, *graphic designer*
Rod Hackney, *Chairman, Inner City Aid*
Gail Hallyburton, *Urban Villages Forum*
Nancy Haque, *Professional Firms Group, Business in the Community*
Nabeel Hamdi, *Director, Centre for Development & Emergency Planning, Oxford Brookes University*
Sue Hargreaves, *John Thompson & Partners*
Brian Hanson, *Director, The Prince of Wales's Project Office*
Lorraine Hart, *Research and Development Officer, The Environment Trust*
Eléonore Hauptmann, *producer of French language version of this manual*
Ian Haywood, *Ian Haywood Partnership*
Amanda Heslop, *Training Officer, Help Age International*
James Hulme, *Director of Public Affairs, The Prince's Foundation*
Richard John, *Director, POWIA*
Joan Kean, *Project Director, Newcastle Architecture Workshop*
Charles Knevitt, *Director, RIBA Trust*
Chris Lakin, *Director, Inner City Aid*
David Lewis, *American Institute of Architects*
Arnold Linden, *Planning Advisory Group, Royal Institute of British Architects*
Caroline Lwin, *Architect*
Charmian Marshall, *Urban Villages Forum*
Eva Nickel, *John Thompson & Partners*
Guy Oliver, *student, POWIA*
Jenneth Parker, *education consultant*
Richard Pullen, *Department of the Environment*
Debbie Radcliffe, *actress and consultant*
Mark Rasmussen, *Researcher, POWIA*
Stephen Reinke, *President, London Chapter, American Institute of Architects*
Jon Rowland, *Chairman, Urban Design Group*
Jane Samuels, *student, POWIA*
Wendy Sarkissian, *author, teacher and consultant, Australia*
Claire Scott, *Research Administrator, POWIA*
Louise Scott, *arts organiser*

Collaborative production
Workshop at an 'Editing Day' held at The Prince of Wales's Institute of Architecture in February 1995. Thirty-three practitioners, designers, editors and potential readers helped to shape the first edition of this book using felt-tip pens on wall mounted page blow-ups; a process adapted from community planning. A similar day was held for this edition. (Clockwise from flipchart: Sue Hargreaves, Rod Hackney, Chris Lakin, Jeremy Caulton, unknown, Debbie Radcliffe, Nick Wates, John Billingham, John Worthington.)

Firas Sharaf, *Assistant Professor, Department of Architecture, University of Jordan*
Alan Simpson, *Urban Design Associates*
Lucien Steil, *The Prince's Foundation*
Sukhvinder Stubbs, *Community Development Manager, English Partnerships*
David Taylor, *Chief Executive, English Partnerships*
Ros Tennyson, *Community Development Consultant, Partnership Unit, Prince of Wales Business Leaders Forum*
John Thompson, *John Thompson & Partners*
John F C Turner, *Architect and writer*
David Turrent, *Architect, ECD architects*
Richard Twinch, *Senior Tutor, POWIA*
Upkar Ubhi, *student, POWIA*

Louise Waring, *Planning Directorate, Communities and Local Government*
Jeremy Wates, *Secretary, Aarhus Convention, UNECE*
Max and Mae Wates, *children (no longer)*
Ted Watts, *Chairman, Watts & Partners*
David Wilcox, *Director, Partnership*
John Worthington, *Director, Institute of Advanced Architectural Studies, University of York, Deputy Chairman, DEGW*
Bob Young, *Chief Executive, Local Space*
Andreas von Zadow, *Community planner, Germany, producer of German and French language version of this manual*
Charles Zucker, *Director, Community Design & Development, American Institute of Architects*

Spreading good practice

How this book has evolved

English, 1996

First edition by **Nick Wates**, **The Prince of Wales's Institute of Architecture**, 1996
ISBN 978-1-898465-11-9
Out of print

Chinese, 1996

Chinese translation by **Ching-Dar Hsieh**, **Chuan Hsing Publishing Company**, 1996
ISBN 978-957-9693-27-1

Tel: +886 2 27752207
Fax: +886 2 27318734
Email: chuanshing@ ms11.url.com.tw

German, 1997

German translation and adaptation by **Andreas von Zadow** with **Bettina Moser** entitled *Perspektiven – werkstatt*, **MATCH**, 1997
ISBN 978-3-88118-231-7
www.matchconsult.de

Sponsors: TrizecHahn, WoGeHe

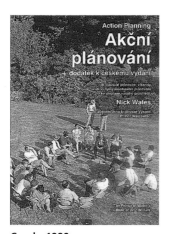

Czech, 1999

English, 2008

French, 2008

Czech translation and adaptation by **Environmental Partnership for Central Europe** – Czech Republic, Program for Public Spaces, 1999 www.environmentalpartnership.org

Sponsor: British Know How Fund

Revised and updated version by **Nick Wates**, Earthscan, 2008 ISBN 978-1-84407-492-1 Introduction by **John Thompson**

Sponsors: The Academy of Urbanism, English Partnerships, John Thompson & Partners, The Prince's Foundation

French translation and adaptation by **Eléonore Hauptmann** with **Andreas von Zadow** entitled *La Participation Dynamique*

Publisher awaited, cover design provisional

Arabic, forthcoming

Arabic translation and adaptation by **Firas Sharaf** Univerisity of Jordan

Photo and Illustration credits

Location, date, and photographer or source of photos and illustrations. Many thanks to all who have allowed their material to be used.

Images identified on page from top down and from left to right. Location in the UK unless otherwise specified

CPW = Community Planning Weekend
JTP = John Thompson & Partners
PF = The Prince's Foundation
NW = Nick Wates

Cover Woking CPW, 2007, JTP; Leverkeusen CPW, Germany, 2000, JTP
iv Pontefract, 2003, NW
ix Upton, 2006, PF (2); Caterham Barracks, 2008, Benedict Luxmoore (2)
xi Poundbury, 1989, PF
xii Leverkeusen CPW, Germany, 2000, JTP
xiii Castleford, 2003, NW
xiv Lübeck CPW, Germany, 2007, Arie Oeveres; Chichester, 2008, JTP
xv Ladder of participation, JTP; Pontefract, 2003, NW
xvii Newcastle, 1998, JTP
xx West Silvertown, London, 1993, unknown
2 unknown, 2007, JTP
5 Caterham Barracks, Surrey, UK, 1998, JTP; Vision drawing for Caterham Barracks, Surrey, 1998, JTP
6 Dickens Yard, CP Event, Ealing, 2007, JTP
7 Cartoon by Louis Hellman, West Silvertown CPW report (page 29), 1993, JTP
8 Topic workshop, Lucan-Clondalkin, Ireland, 2005, JTP; Team opening planning weekend, Lübeck, Germany, 2007, Arie Oeveres
9 Community planning weekends at Cape Hill, Sandwell, 1990, JTP; Poundbury, Dorset, 1989, NW; West Silvertown, London, 1993, NW
12 Steering Group meeting, Lübeck, Germany, 2007, Andreas von Zadow; Client briefing meeting, Sittard-Geleen, Netherlands, 2006, Andreas von Zadow.
14 Chichester CPW, 2008, JTP
18 Regents Park, London, 1995, NW
20 Tower block demolition, London, 1985, NW
22 Planning Weekend set-up, Berger-Levrault, France, 2002, John Thompson
24 Cartoon by Mikhail Riabov, Ludwigsfelde, Germany, 1996

26 Streetlamp banner, Pontefract, Yorkshire, 2003, NW
27 Advertising hoarding, Shankill Road, Belfast, 1995, JTP; publicity leaflets Anderson, Indiana, USA, 1985 and Blairs College, Scotland, 1994.
28 John Thompson & Partners, Aberdeen airport for an event at Blairs College, Scotland, 1994, NW
30 Nancy, France, 2001, JTP
31 Students from Moscow University, ECO 1 Community Planning Event, Russia, 1991, JTP
32 Reinvigorate event, Bristol, 2007, NW
34 Workshop at Reinvigorate event, Bristol, 2007, NW; developer John Muir, Blairs College, Aberdeen, 1994, NW
35 Cuttings: *Birmingham Post,* 1988; *Pittsburgh Press,* 1988; *Sunday Telegraph,* 1989; *Dorset Advertiser,* 1989; *Architects' Journal,* 1990; *Guardian,* 1990; *Southwark Sparrow,* 1993; *Shankill People,* 1995 (a 36-page special issue prior to a planning weekend); *New Start,* 2003
36 Poundbury Planning Weekend, Dorset, 1989, NW; Pontefract Community Planning Event, Yorkshire, 2003, NW
37 Cambridge Stakeholder Participation Day, 2005, NW; Hulme CPW, Manchester, 1992, JTP
38 Cambridge Stakeholder Participation Day, 2003, NW; Workshop on Local Development Framework, Camberley, Surrey, 2006, NW
39 Teamwork, Lübeck, Germany, 2007, Arie Overes
41 Come to the Table conference, Cambourne, Cornwall, 2005, NW; Workshop on Local Development Framework, Camberley, Surrey, 2006, NW
44 Computing, Meppel, Netherlands, 2005, Andreas von Zadow
45 Team working, Lübeck CPW, Germany, 2007, JTP; Draft Masterplan for Aylesham, Kent, 2004, EDAW
46 Report back, Rosyth CPW, 2006, JTP
48 Based on a leaflet for Hulme CPW, Manchester, 1992, JTP
50 Reinvigorate event, Bristol, 2007, NW
62 Heart of East Greenwich collaborative design workshop, 2005, NW
63 Pittsburgh R/UDAT, USA, 1988, JTP; Scarborough CPE, 2002, JTP; Cambridge

Stakeholder Participation Day, 2003, NW; Chichester CPW, 2008, JTP

64 Blairs College CPW, Scotland, 1994, NW

65 Cambridge Southern Fringe stakeholder participation day, 2003, NW

66 Marrowbone Lane CPW, Dublin, 2007, JTP; unknown, 2005, JTP

67 Fair Mile CPW, Cholsey, 2007, JTP; Dickens Yard, CP Event, Ealing, 2007, JTP; Brunswick College Planning day, Cambridge, 2007, JTP

68 Meppel, Pays-Bas, Netherlands, 2005, JTP; Greater Shankill CPW, Belfast, Northern Ireland, 1995, JTP

69 Angell Town CPW, Brixton,1993, JTP; Berger-Levrault, France, 2002, John Thompson; Pittsburgh R/UDAT, 1988, JTP

70 Young people: Pontefract Community Planning Event, Yorkshire, 2003, NW; Aylesham Enquiry by Design, Kent, 2003, EDAW. Aerial photographs: Pontefract Community Planning Event, Yorkshire, 2003, NW. Photos and montages: Heart of East Greenwich collaborative design workshop, 2005, NW

71 Character cards: Workshop on Local Development Framework, Camberley, Surrey, 2006, NW (2). Experts take the lead: Sherford EbD, 2004, PF; Workshop on Local Development Framework, Camberley, Surrey, 2006, NW. Exhibition: Heart of East Greenwich collaborative design workshop, 2005, NW. Flipcharting: Cambridge stakeholder participation day, 2005, NW; Heart of East Greenwich collaborative design workshop, 2005, NW

72 Angell Town CPW, Brixton, 1993, JTP; Pontefract Community Planning Event, Yorkshire, 2003, NW; Heart of East Greenwich collaborative design workshop, 2005, NW

73 Heart of East Greenwich collaborative design workshop, 2005, NW (2); Sherford EbD, 2004, PF; Pontefract Community Planning Event, Yorkshire, 2003, NW

74 Blairs College CPW, Scotland, 1994, NW

75 Sherford Enquiry by Design, 2004, PF (2); Poundbury Planning Weekend, 1989, NW; Blairs College CPW, Scotland, 1994, JTP

76 Poundbury Planning Weekend, 1988, NW; West Silvertown CPW, 1993, NW; Winfrith EbD, 2008, PF

Photographs including flash will be taken

Any images taken here today may be used in future related publications. These in turn could be used for corporate marketing purposes.

Please indicate if you wish not to be photographed

Seeking permission
Sign displayed prominently at an event in an attempt to avoid complaints later on. If anyone is unhappy with appearing in a photo in this book, please send an email to info@nickwates.co.uk identifying the photo and yourself. The photo will then be cropped or removed in future editions.

78-79 Reports and broadsheet from Events in Anderson, Indiana, USA, 1985, AIA; Aylesham, Kent, 2003, Edaw; Sherford, Devon, 2004, PF; Cambridge East, 2005, Nick Wates Associates; Liberties, Dublin, 2007, JTP; Runnymede, Surrey, 2007, JTP; Lübeck, Germany, 2007, von Zadow

80 Blairs College CPW, Scotland, 1994, JTP

81 Poundbury planning weekend, 1989, NW; Lübeck CPW, Germany, 2007, JTP

82 Greater Shankhill CPW, Belfast, 1995, JTP; Sherford Masterplan, 2006, PF

84 Upton, Northampton, 2007, PF

85 Blairs College CPW, Aberdeen, 1994, JTP; Hulme CPW, Manchester, 1992, JTP

86 Upton, Northampton, 2007, PF; Caterham Barracks, Surrey, 2008, JTP

88 Hands-on Planning, Woking CPW, 2007, JTP

91 Map courtesy of The American Institute of Architects

104 Drawings courtesy of von Zadow and JTP

111 The Prince of Wales's Institute of Architecture, London, 1995, Richard Ivey

115 Runnymede CPW, Surrey, 2007

116 unknown, 2007, Arie Ouveres

Quotation credits

Sources and dates of quotations used in this manual.
JTP = interview by John Thompson & Partners
NW = interview by Nick Wates

Index

Index contd.

Index contd.

Index contd.

Nick Wates is a leading authority on community involvement in planning and architecture. As an author, practitioner and teacher he has participated in, and chronicled, its development for over 30 years.

He is Site Editor of *The Community Planning Website* www.communityplanning.net which is based on his popular *Community Planning Handbook* (Earthscan, 2000). Previous books include *Community Architecture* (Penguin, 1987, with Charles Knevitt).

He first experienced a Community Planning Event in 1985 and since then has played a role in dozens – as journalist, observer, coordinator, facilitator, team member, support staff and consultant.

He is director of Nick Wates Associates.

Jeremy Brook is a graphic designer specialising in the design of art publications for museums and art galleries.

He studied at the Royal College of Art and has taught part-time at the London College of Printing, Ravensbourne College of Design, Eastbourne College of Arts and Technology and Hastings College of Arts and Technology.

His clients include: Arts Council England; Chris Beetles Ltd, London; De La Warr Pavilion; RIBA South East; Rye Art Gallery; James Hockey & Foyer Galleries, Farnham; Nick Wates Associates and the University of Westminster.

Previous books include *Erich Mendelsohn 1887–1953* (A3 Times, 1987); *Hans Scharoun: the alternative tradition* (A3 Times, 1995); *Community Planning Handbook* (Earthscan, 2000); *The Rough Guide to Community Asset Management* (University of Westminster, 2005).

He is director of Graphic Ideas.

John Thompson is the Chairman of John Thompson & Partners, one of Europe's leading firms of Architects and Urbanists, and Founder-Chairman of The Academy of Urbanism.

In the 1980s he pioneered the use of Community Planning Events in the United Kingdom as a tool for engaging local people in the design of their own neighbourhoods. Since then he has led a series of seminal projects that have simultaneously delivered physical, social and economic change.

Formerly Chairman of the RIBA Urbanism and Planning Group and a founder member of The Urban Villages Forum, he is currently a member of Yorkshire Forward's Urban and Rural Renaissance Panels.

John has undertaken masterplanning and urban design projects in towns and cities throughout the UK and Europe and is currently designing a series of new settlements in England, Scotland, Iceland and the Moscow City Region.

publishing for a sustainable future

The Community Planning Handbook
How People Can Shape Their Cities,
Towns and Villages in Any Part of the World
Nick Wates

'A very clear, well organized and extremely useful book. With its emphasis on flexibility and adaptation in the face of experience, this is a book that I will recommend to clients and colleagues alike.' *J. Gary Lawrence, President Sustainable Strategies & Solutions, Inc, Seattle*

'An excellent book that will have a host of valuable applications – with sufficient detail for practitioners, researchers, planners and policy makers. It is an important and timely contribution.' *Jules Pretty, Director, Centre for Environment and Society, University of Essex'*

Growing numbers of residents are getting involved with professionals in shaping their local environment, and there is now a powerful range of methods available, from design workshops to electronic maps.

The Community Planning Handbook is the essential starting point for all those involved – planners and local authorities, architects and other practitioners, community workers, students and local residents. It features an accessible how-to-do-it style, best practice information on effective methods, and international scope and relevance.

Tips, checklists and sample documents help readers to get started quickly, learn from others' experience and to select the approach best suited to their situation. The glossary, bibliography and contact details provide quick access to further information and support.

Nick Wates is a writer, researcher and project consultant specializing in community planning and design.

Paperback £18.99 • 236 pages • 978-1-85383-654-1 • 2000

For more details and a full listing of Earthscan titles visit:

www. earthscan .co.uk